TRUE DIVINITY IN CHRIST

ALSO BY JOHN KEITH

Complete Humanity in Jesus: A Theological Memoir

TRUE DIVINITY IN CHRIST

A Testimony of Faith and Hope with Four Short Stories

JOHN M. KEITH

NEWSOUTH BOOKS
Montgomery | Louisville

NewSouth Books
105 South Court Street
Montgomery, AL 36104

Library of Congress Cataloging-in-Publication Data

Keith, John M.
True divinity in Christ : a testimony of faith and hope with four short stories
/ John M. Keith.

p. cm.

ISBN-13: 978-1-60306-057-8
ISBN-10: 1-60306-057-X

1. Christian life. 2. Jesus Christ—Divinity.
3. Christian fiction, American. I. Title.
BV4501.3.K445 2010
248—dc22

2010023049

Printed in the United States of America

FOR MY WIFE, RILLA,
AND MY DAUGHTER, LAUREN

CONTENTS

Introduction

"We have confidence to enter the sanctuary by the blood of Jesus, by the new and living way that he opened to us through the curtain, that is through his flesh." — HEBREWS 10:19–20

The genre of this book might be called "confessional theology." In any case it is my own testimony, but it does not cover everything I believe about God. It is more an expression of my personal faith and hope than a systematic and philosophical inquiry. Although not technical or academic theology, the book does reflect my study and critical thinking. It is also drawn from the experiences of my life, especially in prayer, worship, and observation of other people in churches from my infancy into my retirement. The meditations of this book begin with how God becomes known to us. They progress to how we are transformed by God, how we may share in the life of God, and how we may participate in the work of God in the world.

The four chapters that follow are titled "Epiphany," "Transfiguration," "Resurrection," and "Ascension." Although they will explore some of the biblical events in Jesus's life to which these titles refer, they are used here more typologically to meditate on the journey of faith from knowing God (or more accurately being known by God) to being transformed by God, to sharing in the life of God to participating in the work of God. In a similar manner references will be made to the celebrations of Epiphany, Transfiguration, Resurrection, and Ascension in the liturgy of the church, but the emphasis again will be on the spiritual experiences of individual people and of Christian people in community.

Because the sacraments of the church (baptism, communion, confirmation, marriage, ordination, reconciliation of penitents, and anointing of the sick) symbolize and incorporate many of these spiritual experiences, they will also be related to epiphany, transfiguration, resurrection, and ascension, as the titular categories I have chosen for the description of God's encounter and involvement with us.

I will use a format that juxtaposes an expository text with stories about people who lived during my lifetime from the mid-twentieth century to the early twenty-first century. In my earlier book, *Complete Humanity in Jesus: A Theological Memoir*, the expository text alternated with autobiographical vignettes, but in this book short stories about other people follow the theological musing. Some of these stories are drawn from composite characters of people whom I have known during my ministry in a variety of parishes and congregations but are adapted and altered by my imagination. Likewise some events have roots in things that happened, but all are greatly changed, and many are created out of pure fantasy.

These stories are not meant to illustrate the themes of epiphany, transfiguration, resurrection, and ascension but rather to resonate with them. It is my hope that in these narratives, as in daily life, an intimation of the divine presence may be glimpsed, although the sighting is always veiled and often ambiguous. I had intended that more explicit references to the sacraments might be suggested in the stories and that they might resonate in a particular way with each of the titular categories. Alas, as any writer of fiction knows, the characters and events of a narrative take on their own lives as they develop and escape the preordained boundaries the author had set for them. So it is that each of the stories may have certain resonating chords with all of the "Epiphany," "Transfiguration," "Resurrection," and "Ascension" chapters, but perhaps with one or another more than with others.

Although I have attempted to reflect accurately events in church history and to use modern exegetical methods in discussing biblical texts, this book is the work of a retired village parson. I do not claim that it is a scholarly tome, and it should not be judged or read as such. The same tools and methods I tried to use faithfully in preparing sermons for more than half a century are employed here, but I have tried not to "preach," as that word is often interpreted negatively. Instead, the book as a whole, including the stories, represents my personal testimony of faith and hope.

As a Christian I affirm that God acts to become known to me particularly in Jesus Christ. The "how" of that becoming known is difficult to fathom, but somehow it entails divinity revealed within humanity. In *Complete Humanity in Jesus*, I sought to express the personal meaning of how I am aware of my own humanity in relation to Jesus. The prepositions used in the titles of both books are important: Complete Humanity *in* Jesus and True Divinity *in* Christ rather than Complete Humanity *of* Jesus and True Divinity *of* Christ.

What follows in this introduction quotes some rather difficult and archaic material from the history of early theologians. I believe that working through these quotations can provide a helpful background for the chapters that follow, which I hope will be more easily accessible. Those readers who will slog through the technical theological words and phrases should be rewarded with a historical basis for understanding the thesis of this book.

Although it is necessary to explore Jesus's humanity and Christ's divinity as a beginning, my focus in the former book was on how we find our own humanity in relationship to Jesus. Here the focus will be on how we participate in the life of God by our relationship to Christ. It is my belief that in a Christian context of discourse, divinity cannot be contemplated unless one begins with humanity. We must first see Jesus's humanity and then see divinity "through it." The metaphor of a stained-glass window is a cliché, but it expresses about as well as any metaphor can how the light of divine presence is refracted through the flesh of a man.

In searching for the meaning of our humanity by contemplating the full, perfect, complete humanity of Jesus, my earlier book sought a theological foundation in the "Definition of the Union of the Divine and Human Natures in the Person of Christ" formulated at the Council of Chalcedon in A.D. 451. In my search for the divinity of Christ I turn to the same theological statement. "Our Lord Jesus Christ, at once complete in Godhead and complete in manhood, truly God and truly man consisting also of a reasonable soul and body [*en teleion ton auton Thetati, teleion ton auton en anthropotati, Theon alethos kai anthropon alethos ton auton ek psyches logikes kai somatos*]; of one substance [*homoousios*] with the Father as regards his Godhead, and at the same time one substance [*homoousios*] with us as regards his manhood; like us in all respects apart from sin."[1]

In the former book the emphasis was on the complete humanity of Jesus. This book begins with a focus on the true divinity of Jesus, but my meditation will not be confined to pondering how Christ is fully God but will soon proceed to the mystery of how his divinity affects us because he was also completely human. In other words, it is not so much Christ's human nature in itself or Christ's divine nature in itself but rather the "union," as noted above in the Definition of Chalcedon, that will be the principal concern. Jesus Christ is not only the reference point for knowing God as he reveals the true nature of God in human form, but Jesus Christ is also the source of grace through whom we are transformed (or "conformed" to his image) and through whom we attain the gifts of sharing God's life and work in the world, especially as we encounter him as the Risen Lord.

My former book began and ended with paraphrases of quotations from Ireneaus, the second-century Bishop of Lyon, who was arguably the first great post-biblical theologian and more certainly the first great theologian of the Western world. The concluding quote from Irenaeus clearly enunciated the almost absurdly radical claim at the heart of Christian faith that "Christ became human, so that human beings might become divine"—or more accurately translated, "Christ became what we are in order to enable us to become what he is."[2]

Before pondering the second part of Irenaeus's dictum, "how we might become what Christ is," which will be the principal focus of this book, the first part must be considered, "how Christ became what we are." "Incarnation" is the theological word for Christ's becoming human as we are. In *Against Heresies*, Irenaeus wrote that "if the flesh were not in a position to be saved, the Word of God would certainly not have become flesh."[3] Thus Irenaeus had a favorable estimation of humanity, despite its having been marred by sin. He might have been closer to the view of Pelagius, who believed that despite having fallen into a sinful state, human beings retained some traces of innate goodness and soundness, than he was to Augustine who believed that the human race was totally depraved through original sin. Their controversies, however, belong to a time hundreds of years after Irenaeus with its own descriptions and distinctions.

Irenaeus wrote that "the only-begotten Word, who is always present with the human race, united and mingled with his handiwork, according to the Father's pleasure, and incarnate, is himself Jesus Christ our Lord, who suffered for us, and rose again for us, and is to come in the glory of the Father to raise all flesh to manifest salvation, and to apply the rule of just judgment to all who were made by him . . . Christ Jesus our Lord . . . came in fulfillment of God's comprehensive design and consummates all thing in himself: he was invisible and became visible; incomprehensible and made comprehensible; the Word, and made man, *consummating all things in himself*."[4] Irenaeus was even reported to have said, "The glory of God is humanity fully alive."[5]

Several centuries later the dogma summarizing the two natures of Christ in one person in the (so-called) Athanasian Creed affirmed, "Our Lord Jesus Christ . . . is one, not because his divinity was changed into flesh, but because his humanity was *assumed unto God* [*sed assumptione humanitatis in Deum*]."[6]

The extension of the idea of Christ's humanity being assumed unto God to the idea of our being assumed unto God will be explored in the following chapters. The Apostle Paul was perhaps the first to enunciate this idea of incarnational redemption. He wrote to the church in Corinth, "Just as we have borne the image of the man of dust, we will also bear the image of the man of heaven" (II Corinthians 15:44). The sentiment is echoed in II Peter 1:4, which assures ". . . his precious and very great promises . . . [that you] may become participants of the divine nature."[7] A century after Paul and Peter, Irenaeus filled out their seminal suggestions. Perhaps no theologian before or since Irenaeus has more fully associated the whole of Christ's life and work, his teaching and healing as well as his death and resurrection, with the salvation of the world. "He [Christ] caused man [humanity] to cleave to and become one with God. For unless man had overcome the enemy of man, the enemy would not have been legitimately vanquished."[8]

Rather than the philosophically precise and the difficult to understand terms and phrases used by theologians during the following couple of centuries as they sought to define the two natures and one person of Christ, Irenaeus wrote about incarnational salvation in language that is eloquent and poetic. "For there is one Son who accomplished the Father's will and one human race in [which] the mysteries, i.e., the divine purposes of God, are fulfilled, 'whom angels long to see,' and are not able to search out the wisdom of God, whereby his handiwork is perfected by being conformed to the Son and incorporated in him; namely that his offspring, the first-begotten Word, should descend into creation, into his handiwork, and be received thereby; that creation, for its part, should receive the Word and ascend to him rising above the angels, to be made according to the image and likeness of God."[9]

For the next two centuries theologians elaborated the idea of incarnational redemption from the suggestions of Peter and Paul and Irenaeus. Although the death of Jesus on the cross was a major event (even *the* major event) in the salvation story related by Paul and Irenaeus, the crucifixion came more and more to be seen as the only cause of human redemption in succeeding centuries. In the debates over a century after Irenaeus wrote *Adversus Haereses* about how the incarnated Christ was related to God the Father, Athanasius was the leading theologian whose views prevailed as the accepted doctrine of the Church. Almost echoing the words of Irenaeus, Athanasius wrote, "The Word was made man in order that we might be made divine."[10] He expounded more fully, "The Word begotten of the Father from on high, inexpressibly, inexplicably, incomprehensibly, and eternally, is he that is born in time here below, of the Virgin Mary, the Mother of God—so that those who are in the first place born here below might have a second birth from on high, that is, from God."[11]

In another book Athanasius again echoed Irenaeus by explaining that, "He [Christ] assumed a created human body, that, having renewed it as its creator, he might deify it in himself, and thus bring us all into the kingdom of heaven through our likeness to him . . . We should not have been freed from sin and the curse, had not the flesh which the Word assumed been by nature human (for we should have nothing in common with what is alien to us); so too humanity would not have been deified, if the Word who became flesh had not been derived from the Father and his true and proper Word."[12]

Beginning with Athanasius, however, and continuing throughout the Medieval and Reformation periods, the emphasis in the salvation story increasingly emphasized the cross and the death of Jesus to the exclusion of everything else. In the same book echoing the words of Irenaeus, Athanasius affirmed that "The Word takes to himself a body capable of death, that it, by partaking of the Word, who is above all, might be worthy to die in the stead of all, and might because of the Word which was come to dwell in it, remain incorruptible, and that thenceforth corruption might be stayed from all by the grace of the resurrection."[13]

Progressively from the fourth century until the eleventh century the cross and death of Jesus became almost exclusively the event of redemption for the human race until Anselm expounded a theory of substitutionary sacrifice by Christ for us on the cross in *Cur Deus Homo*, reasoning that the only reason for the divine to become human was so that the incarnated Christ could be put to death in our stead. While in the Western Church this dominant concentration on the crucifixion prevailed, the Eastern Church maintained an understanding of salvation through the complete incarnation of Christ, which is sometimes called a mystical or physical account of atonement.[14]

To be sure, the expression of incarnational salvation enunciated by Irenaeus was revived even in the Western Church at various times. A century after Athanasius, Pope Leo the Great reiterated the insights of Irenaeus by stating that "the Son of God became the Son of Man that sons of man might become sons of God." During this era a collect for the Christmas season was incorporated into the Leonine Sacramentary of the early seventh century and echoed in the Gelasian Sacramentary, eventually finding its way into *The Book of Common Prayer*. It is appointed for two purposes in the present American version, for the Second Sunday after Christmas Day and for various other occasions celebrating the Incarnation: "O God, who wonderfully created, and yet more wonderfully restored the dignity of human nature: Grant that we may share the divine life of him who humbled himself to share our humanity, your Son Jesus Christ . . ."[15] In the revision of *The Book of Common Prayer* in 1662 a collect was also added that included a plea that ". . . we may be made like unto him [Christ] in his eternal and glorious kingdom."[16]

The concept of incarnational salvation was expressed again more frequently in the nineteenth and early twentieth centuries, especially in the writings of Albert Schweitzer.

Although Albert Schweitzer may be better known for *The Quest for the Historical Jesus*,[17] in which he portrayed Jesus as an apocalyptic teacher, he recognized the contrast between the soteriology (salvation story) in how the Eastern Church drew its life from mysticism and how the Western Church, especially in its Protestant denominations after the Reformation, concentrated on the doctrine of justification.[18] Schweitzer's question, "Who was Jesus historically?" may be more relevant to theological inquiries down to the theories of Marcus Borg, John Dominic Crossan, et al., and the "Jesus Seminar" today than Schweitzer's answers. His discourses in *The Mysticism of Paul the Apostle*, however, written several decades after *The Quest for the Historical Jesus*, are as fresh and relevant today as they were in the early twentieth century. He grasps the essence of incarnational salvation that "alongside the 'we in Christ' there occurs the converse 'Christ in us.'"[19] He summarized the thesis elaborated in this book with the same kind of eloquent brevity found in Irenaeus. "The being-in-Christ in itself signified a partaking, even though still hidden, in the heavenly corporeity of Christ."[20]

It is both heretical and unhistorical to use "Jesus" to refer to the human nature and to use "Christ" to refer to the divine nature. Historically "Christ" was a Greek translation of the Jewish title "Messiah," but because references to a Jewish "Messiah" had little meaning in those parts of the church dominated by Gentiles, "Christ" began to be used from the time of Paul's letters onward almost like a second name. In more recent centuries some theologians have made a distinction between the "Jesus of history" and the "Christ of faith."[21]

In the following pages I often use "Christ" to refer to the Risen Lord and "Jesus" to refer to the incarnate Savior who was born, lived, and died before the first Easter day, but I do not intend any separation or distinction between Jesus and Christ—both refer equally to the same person and to the two natures of the one Lord. As was the case in the meditation from my former book, when I was focusing on the human nature of Jesus but did not want in any way to deny the divine nature of Christ, the same caution must be observed here, as I reverse the words "human" and "divine" that I wrote then. "Although the emphasis of the meditation here will be on the 'divine' [human] nature of Christ, there is no intention to deny or compromise the 'human' [divine] nature of Christ. It may be difficult (but very necessary and important at all times) to avoid the implication of failing to recognize the 'two natures, without division, without separation.'"[22]

The insights of Schweitzer, Athanasius, Irenaeus, and, of course, the Apostle Paul and the Creeds of the church will be met again and quoted in the inquiries that follow: What does it mean to bear the image of Christ? How might we be assumed unto God by the incarnation and atonement of Christ? Can a process be discerned and described for becoming "we in Christ" and "Christ in us"? These are some of the questions that will occupy the attention of the remainder of this book.

Notes

1   Greek and translation from William Bright, *The Canons of the First Four General Councils*, second edition, Oxford University Press, 1892, pp. xxxii-xxxvi.

2   William C. Placher, "How Does Jesus Save?' *The Christian Century*, vol. 126, no. 11, July 2, 2009, p. 26. Henry Bettenson renders the quotation as "Our

Lord Jesus Christ, the Word of God, of his boundless love became what we are that he might make us what he himself is" in *The Early Christian Fathers*, Oxford University Press, 1956, p. 106. John Willis translates: ". . . through His transcendent love, [Christ] became what we are, that He might bring us to be even what He is Himself" (*The Teaching of the Church Fathers*, Herder and Herder, 1966, p. 342). The quotation is found in the preface to book five of Irenaeus's *Adversus Haereses*.

3   W. A. Jurgens, *The Faith of the Early Fathers*, The Liturgical Press, 1970, p. 101. The quotation is from *Adversus Haereses*, book five, chapter 14.1.

4   Bettennson, pp.110–111. The quotation is from book two, chapter xxii.4. (Italics in the English translation are added by me to offer emphasis for the premise of this book.)

5   Thomas L. Long, "Living by the Word," *The Christian Century*, vol. 123, no. 6, March 21, 2006, p. 19.

6   Latin and translation from "Quicumque Athanasian Creed," www.creeds. net/ancient/Quincumque. (Italics in the English translation are added to offer emphasis for the premise of this book.) See also the translation, "Quicunque Vult commonly called The Creed of St. Athanasius," in *The Book of Common Prayer*, The Episcopal Church, The Church Hymnal Corporation and the Seabury Press, 1979, pp. 864–865. Modern scholars believe that the Creed was formulated about a century after the lifetime of St. Athanasius, probably in Gaul rather than in Alexandria. For a fuller details see *The Oxford English Dictionary of the Christian Church*, F. L. Cross, editor, Oxford University Press, 1958, pp. 98–99.

7   The translation in the King James Version reads "that ye might be partakers of the divine nature." All citations in this book are from the New Revised Standard Version unless otherwise noted.

8   Willis, p. 317 The quotation is from book three, chapter xviii.7.

9   Bettenson, p. 140. The quotation is from book three, chapter xxxvi.3.

10   Ibid. p. 404. The quotation is from *De Incarnatione* 54.

11   Jurgens, p. 340.

12   Bettenson, p. 404. The quotation is from *Contra Arianos* ii.70.

13   Thomas G. Weinandy, *Athanasius: A Theological Introduction*, Ashgate, 2007, p. 33. The quotation is from *De Incarnatione*, chapter 9.1.

14   Plancher, p. 27.

15   Marion T. Hatchett, *Commentary on the American Prayer Book*, The Seabury Press, New York, 1981, p. 170. Although the eminent liturgical scholar elucidates the background for the collect, he mistakenly gives Leo the Great credit for originating the sentiment expressed by Irenaeus three

centuries earlier. The collect is found in *The Book of Common Prayer*, pp. 162, 200, 214, and 252.

16 The collect was appointed for the Sixth Sunday after the Epiphany and is attributed to Bishop John Cousin. Although it was still used on the Sixth Sunday after the Epiphany in the *American Prayer Book of 1928*, it was transferred to the Sunday following Pentecost closest to November 9 in the revision of 1979. Ibid. p. 195.

17 Translated by W. Montgomery, A & C Black, 1910.

18 Albert Schweitzer, *The Mysticism of Paul the Apostle*, A & C Black, 1931, revised edition Seabury, 1968, p. 391.

19 Ibid. p. 122.

20 Ibid. p. 134.

21 The phrase "The Jesus of history and the Christ of faith" was coined in 1892 by Martin Kähler. It has been used in one way or another by theologians from Frederich Schleiermacher to Albert Schweitzer to Rudolf Bultmann to Ernst Käseman down to Marcus Borg and the "Jesus Seminar" of recent years. For a fuller discussion see "The Jesus of History and the Christ of Faith: Some Contemporary Reflections," lecture at Yorkminster Park Baptist Church, Toronto, Canada, February 11, 1999, www.macmaster.ca/mjtm/2-51.

22 Definition of the "Union of the Divine and Human Natures in the Person of Christ," *The Book of Common Prayer*, p. 864. The quotation is from my earlier book, *The Complete Humanity of Jesus: A Theological Memoir*, NewSouth Books, 2009, p. 10.

Epiphany

"The grace was given to us in Christ Jesus before the ages began, but it has now been revealed through the 'appearing' [epiphaneia in Greek] of our Savior Jesus Christ, who brought life and immortality to light through the Gospel." — II TIMOTHY 1:9–10

An epiphany in religious parlance can be described broadly as any human encounter with a divine presence. Almost every human being who has ever lived on the planet has experienced epiphanies. Even the most convinced atheist has very likely undergone moments when emotions and thoughts were aroused by something that seemed beyond empirical and rational explanation.

What we do with our epiphanies makes them important in shaping our lives. They may be dismissed as mere illusions and never have much impact on us. They may be cherished as magical fantasies that distract us from an engagement in reality. They may be accepted as literal versions of truth, which may lead to dangerous and harmful responses. Or they may be interpreted in the context of a religious faith that relates them to the epiphanies of other people down through the centuries and places them alongside other guides for spiritual understanding.

In a religious context of understanding, an epiphany always involves self-awareness, oftentimes a new awareness of the self that leads to a fuller self-understanding. This self-awareness usually precedes the awareness of a divine presence, although an acknowledgement of a divine presence distinguishes an epiphany from other experiences of self-understanding. An epiphany is also distinguished from a theophany by the importance of self-awareness rather than the exclusive emphasis on a sense of divine presence. These two elements are always present together in epiphanies as described in this chapter: self-awareness and a sense of divine presence.

Other aspects can be discerned in the stories of epiphanies that are recorded in the Bible. The epiphany may be understood and interpreted and recorded after the event, sometimes a long time after it has been experienced. Epiphanies do not necessarily belong to a particular religious faith. Although the meaning of an epiphany may be interpreted in the context of a particular religion, the experience itself may precede and often comes from outside a faith tradition even for those inured in it. Even in the discussion of Christ as the ultimate epiphany for Christians that follows below, it is well to remember that epiphanies do not belong just to Christianity nor even just to the Abrahamic traditions of faith. The stories of biblical epiphanies are most distinctive, however, in their usual inclusion of a particular kind of promise—a promise that involves a vocation.

From the patriarchs to the prophets, the Hebrew scriptures are replete with stories of epiphanies that illustrate both the themes that are shared with all religious epiphanies and also the qualities that make them distinctive. Abraham was often visited by messengers from God, notably by the three angelic visitors at the oaks of Mamre (Genesis 18:1–21). The dreams of Joseph may have undergone a romantic retelling, but they also represent a certain type of epiphany (Genesis 37–50). The story of Joseph illustrates a growing spiritual maturity from an arrogant, self-centered youth to a compassionate, merciful adult, a progression in faith that will be explored more fully in the next chapter, titled "Transfiguration."

One of the iconic narratives of an epiphany in the Bible describes the experience of the child Samuel at the Hebrew shrine of Shiloh (I Samuel 3:2–9). Samuel's epiphany begins, as most do, with an awareness of himself. His answer to the voice calling his name in his dream or vision was "here am I." He was a child, still untutored in religious language and tradition, thus demonstrating that epiphanies do not necessarily belong to a particular religious faith. God promised in Samuel's epiphany to do a new and great thing in Israel, and Samuel was called to be a prophet to pronounce God's message of justice and righteousness. It was also promised, perhaps later, that none of Samuel's words would "fall to the ground" (I Samuel 3:19). Like most biblical descriptions of epiphanies, this story was recorded and interpreted much later, but it retains the freshness of the spontaneous experience of a child. Four times during the night the boy was awakened by what he believed to be a voice calling his name. He mistook it for a human voice and ran to awaken his teacher, Eli. After the third such rousing, the old prophet Eli suggested to the boy that the words he was hearing might be a message from God.

Moses to some extent and Isaiah to a much greater extent were familiar with a particular religious tradition when their archetypal epiphanies happened. However, the burning bush and the vision in the Temple may not have been the first times that Moses and Isaiah were encountered by a divine presence. A sequence of epiphanies is part of what happens when a life is transformed, as will be the subject of the next chapter, where Moses's life is further discussed.

The familiar account of Moses's epiphany at the burning bush includes some of the same aspects that were noted in the experience of the child Samuel. God called out from the burning bush, "Moses, Moses!" and Moses became self-aware, "Here I am." This self-awareness was followed by a sense of the holy; Moses removed his shoes, and God was revealed and recounted historical events and ancestors and ethical empathy: "I have observed the suffering of my people." In the following chapter of Exodus the call to vocation and the divine promise are enunciated and elaborated where Yahweh promises to be with Moses and give Moses the words that his brother Aaron will speak for him as they serve God together (Exodus 3–4).

Unlike the boy Samuel and the refugee Moses, Isaiah had attained both advanced age and a position of high rank in the state and the religion (which were inseparable in that era) by the time he experienced his famous epiphany. The five chapters that precede Isaiah's epiphany in his recorded prophecy perhaps symbolize his religious involvement before his vision of the Lord in the Temple. He had been something like a "secretary of state" for King Uzziah, and the death of King Uzziah provided the background for his epiphany, as critical events often precede and perhaps induce epiphanal experiences. The new self-understanding of Isaiah is dramatic: "Woe is me! I am lost, for I am a man of unclean lips, and I live in the midst of a people of unclean lips"—followed by a vision of God—". . . my eyes have seen the King, the Lord of hosts!" (Isaiah 6:5). Then Isaiah is called to a new vocation along with its attendant promise and message.

Centuries before Isaiah and even before Samuel, Jacob had experienced an epiphany in his famous dream of angelic messengers descending and ascending a stairway to heaven, and he expressed a vision of God in sentiments much like Isaiah's: "Surely God is in this place . . . How awesome in this place! This is none other than the house of God, and this is the gate of heaven" (Genesis 28:16–18). In a later epiphany, together with a new purpose and a new mission, Jacob is given a new identity and a new name, Israel. A new name often accompanies a new purpose as a motif found in many biblical epiphany stories (Genesis 32:28).

People encounter God in many and various ways in the Hebrew scriptures, even through a conversation with a donkey (Numbers 22:22–30). Epiphanies are also varied and diverse for people in later centuries and even for people today, but in the Christian faith all epiphanies are understood and interpreted by the ultimate epiphany (manifestation) of Jesus Christ, especially by their encounters with the Risen Christ.

The Greek word "epiphaneia" occurs only six times in the New Testament, and all of them have eschatological or apocalyptic references except for the quotation from II Timothy that heads this chapter.[1] This quotation from II Timothy describes a grace given to us by God before all ages. Although the grace given before the world began could be (and has been) interpreted to refer to the predestination of the elect ("us"), it can be read as grace given in Christ to all people of all places and times ("us") which is brought to light by the appearance (epiphany) of Jesus and is appropriated by us in an encounter with him through the Gospel. It is significant that in Christian faith an epiphany does not so much involve the origination of God's grace but rather brings it to light, uncovers it, manifests it, creates the conditions that allow it to be received. Those phrases, "brings to light," "uncovers," "manifests," and "creates conditions for reception," could all be used as definitions for epiphany.

In elucidating the primary setting for the epiphanies of Christians in their encounters with Jesus Christ, John's Gospel will be a primary resource. In the quest for understanding the full and complete humanity of Jesus described in my previous book, the Synoptic Gospels (Matthew, Mark, and Luke) were the dominant guides. They begin with the perfect man, Jesus, and show how people are led to see God embodied in him. John begins with an affirmation of God who became a human being.

The contrast between the first verse of Matthew and the first verse of John could not be more definitive. Matthew begins with "an account of Jesus the Messiah, the Son of David, the son of Abraham," and Mark and Luke have similar introductions. John's Gospel opens with the statement, "In the beginning was the Word, and the Word was with God, and the Word was God," and later affirms that "the Word became flesh and lived among us" (John 1:1, 14).

John's Gospel may thus be described, especially in its first chapters, as a collection of epiphany stories. It is my opinion that John relates events as if what transpired could be seen at that moment in the full knowledge and perspective of the Risen Christ.[2] To be sure, Matthew, Mark, and Luke all know how the story will end. They seek, however, to recount the events that led up to the Resurrection at the time of their occurrence, even though anticipations and predictions of outcomes are included in their narratives. Luke enunciates his goal to "set down an orderly account of the events that have been fulfilled among us just as they were handed down to us by those who from the beginning were eyewitnesses" (Luke 1:1–2).

Encounters with Jesus from the perspective of Mark's Gospel contrast greatly with the perspective of John's Gospel. Mark is noted for what scholars for many years have called "the Messianic secret." Only the demons recognize who Jesus truly is before the completion of his mission in his death and resurrection, and Jesus does not allow them to speak and reveal his true identity. In John's Gospel humble and un-tutored people often recognize the divine identity of Jesus while those of great learning and piety do not know who he truly is.[3]

As recorded in the Synoptic Gospels, encounters of people with Jesus depict how people met a man in whom many began to see glimpses of a holy presence. John's Gospel depicts everyone's meeting with Jesus as an encounter with God incarnated in human form, whether they were fully aware of his divinity or not. Thus John's Gospel can be a guidebook for understanding the meaning of a Christian epiphany, that is, what it entails for people to see God in Christ. Two encounters will be highlighted from the fourth Gospel: the call of the disciple—later apostle—Nathanael, and the meeting with the Samaritan woman at Jacob's well.

In his first meeting with Nathanael, Jesus reveals Nathanael's iden-tity to himself, "An Israelite indeed in whom is no guile." To which Nathanael responds, "How do you know me?" (John 1:47–48 RSV). The very nature of an epiphany entails the recognition of oneself, often the surprising revelation of something new and startling about oneself, before the revelation of deity. Nathanael's recognition of Christ and affirmation of faith that follow his self-recognition are among the most dramatic and eloquent expressions in an epiphany of a first encounter with Christ. "Rabbi, you are the Son of God! You are the King of Israel!" (John 1:49 RSV).

The explicit call to discipleship—the vocational aspect of an epiphany—is not enunciated in the account of the meeting of Jesus and Nathanael, although it follows the call of Philip, which had in turn followed the call of the four fishing partners, Andrew, Peter, James, and John, and it is assumed that Nathanael also became a disciple. Not every aspect is included in every epiphany, and not every aspect that may have been involved in an epiphany is included in every account, but self-recognition and an encounter with deity are always present and usually recorded in Christian epiphanies.

John concludes the account of Nathanael's encounter with Jesus, however, with an explicit promise, "You will see the heaven opened, and the angels of God ascending and descending on the Son of man" (John 1:51 RSV). The pronoun "you" is here rendered as a plural, epitomizing John's practice of universalizing an epiphany story as a guide for other believers who will meet Christ.

Jesus's encounter with the Samaritan woman at Jacob's well is much longer and more complex than his encounter with Nathanael. In fact, it is the longest account of any meeting with Jesus in the New Testament, and so John tells the story as a model for all Christian epiphanies. The significance of the woman's ancestry as a Samaritan cannot be overlooked. In the Synoptic Gospels as well as in John, people whose faith is commended by Jesus are often those who are outcasts, those marginalized, those outside the religious or social inner circles, tax collectors, prostitutes, those too poor to observe proper rituals. Samaritans were the most suspected and even despised of all, for historical and religious reasons.[4]

After the witness of John the Baptist to Jesus as the Lamb of God and the call of several of the most well known disciples (later apostles) in the first chapter and an excursus in the second chapter about Jesus's first miracle at the wedding feast in Cana (which will be mentioned briefly later) and the meeting with Nicodemus, who was a leader in the political and religious establishment in the third chapter, John spends most of the fourth chapter detailing Jesus's meeting with the Samaritan woman, who represents a dramatic contrast to the aristocratic Nicodemus.

The encounter begins with a request for a drink of water, and it suggests that epiphanies often occur in the humdrum activities of daily life. Then Jesus and the woman banter back and forth with a dialogue that might have been lifted from pick-up lines in a bar scripted for a TV sitcom. Of course Jesus is not only whetting the woman's curiosity but also drawing her more and more deeply into a spiritual understanding, first by speaking about "living water" and then by suggesting that those who drink the water that he can provide will never be thirsty again. The woman takes the bait. She is intrigued, but also spiritually "thirsty" in the metaphorical language that Jesus is using and John is employing in telling the story. Then Jesus springs the trap door of the epiphany experience: "Go, call your husband," to which the woman responds, "I have no husband."

The woman is revealed to herself and then almost immediately recognizes a spiritual aura in Jesus. "Sir, I see that you are a prophet." Here John telescopes the narratives of the synoptic Gospel accounts into one encounter, as the woman is led to see Jesus first as a prophet, then as the Messiah, after which she was commissioned with the vocation of telling the people of her village about her epiphany. She reflected back on her experience, affirming that Jesus had "told her everything she had ever done"—in other words that he had revealed her completely to herself, a primary part of a biblical epiphany.

When Jesus's disciples returned they expressed their astonishment that he was speaking not only with a Samaritan but also with a woman. Both of these were categories of people outside the conventional discourse allowed under the religious and political restrictions of the time and so implicitly outside the context of a particular religion. Thus all the aspects of epiphanies, as they are described in the Bible, are exhibited in this story: self-awareness, progressive awareness of deity, promise, vocation, interpretation of meanings after the event, and occurrence outside a particular religious tradition.

Christian tradition brings new and enhanced meanings to the term epiphany (*epiphaneia*) in liturgical worship. The Feast of the Epiphany originated in the Eastern Church and became a dominant celebration by the third century. It was revered as one of three principal feasts, together with Pentecost and Easter. Only later was the Feast of the Epiphany associated with the Magi (Wise Men) as the "manifestation" (epiphany) of Christ to the Gentiles. The Western Church began to associate the Feast of the Epiphany with Jesus's birth, an event not part of the original celebration of the East (and even later the celebration of Jesus's birth was removed from the Feast of the Epiphany in the West and made the separate celebration of Nativity or Christmas). In the fifth century Pope Leo the Great attempted to change the designation of the liturgical feast from "Epiphany" to "Theophany." Fortunately, the change did not stick, because as noted above, epiphany involves many other aspects besides the appearance of God (or gods).[5]

The liturgical season of Epiphany always includes several events from the life of Jesus and the early church that contribute to the understanding of the spiritual experience of epiphany which is the principal concern of this chapter. Of course, the Feast of the Epiphany in the Western Church features the Wise Men, whose quest of faith as Gentiles symbolizes the opening of the biblical promise to peoples of all nations and races. The confession of Peter that Jesus is the Messiah, the Son of God, at Caesarea Philippi was surely a momentous epiphany, and the conversion, more accurately described as an epiphany, of Paul on the Damascus Road is probably the archetypal epiphany in Christian memory. It is appropriate that the feasts commemorating those consummate events always fall for deliberate reasons during the liturgical season of Epiphany.

Paul's famous epiphany on the Damascus Road was initiated, as most epiphanies are, with a command to acknowledge his self-awareness. "Saul, Saul, why do you persecute me?" (Saul was later named Paul, as new names were often given in connection with a significant epiphany.) He immediately recognized a divine presence, "Who are you, Lord?" And the divine presence identified himself as Jesus. Unlike the Old Testament epiphanies that were noted earlier, however, the call to a new vocation and the divine promise were deliberately deferred until later: ". . . enter the city [Damascus], and you will be told what to do" (Acts 9:3–6). [6] (This process of progressive revelation will be explored more fully in the next chapter, "Transfiguration.")

In some periods of history the wedding feast at Cana was associated with the Epiphany season, where Jesus performed his first miracle or "sign" revealing his divine identity. In the contemporary lectionary of most Western churches, the call of the disciples is featured in the Gospel readings during the early weeks of the Epiphany season and thereby the themes of vocation and mission are introduced. The Presentation of Jesus in the Temple for his circumcision on the eighth day after his birth is also celebrated during the season of Epiphany. In several of his writings Augustine of Hippo notes the parallels between the Hebrew ritual of circumcision and the Christian sacrament of baptism. He even calls baptism "spiritual circumcision" in one of his letters.[7] At the event of Jesus's circumcision in the Temple the old priest Simeon gave thanks for not dying until he had seen the Lord's Messiah (Luke 2:26). "Seeing the Christ" is once again a good definition for a Christian experience of epiphany.

From the beginning in the East, the Feast of the Epiphany was associated especially with Jesus's baptism as the focus of his appearance and manifestation as God revealed in human form. Now the commemoration of Jesus's baptism is recalled on the Sunday following the Feast of the Epiphany in the Western Church. People sometimes puzzle over the relationship between Jesus's baptism and the sacrament of baptism in the Church. Jesus was sinless, and part of the symbolism of Christian baptism involves the washing away of sin and the renunciation of evil. Even in the biblical account John the Baptist questions the purpose of Jesus's being baptized, saying that he needs to be baptized by Jesus and asking why Jesus is coming to him (Matthew 3:14). Yet, Jesus's baptism was the "announcement" of his identity as "perfect God, perfect man"[8] and Christian baptism is the pronouncement of our truest identity. For Christians, baptism is the pattern by which all epiphanies are understood, and the baptism of Jesus is the most important event celebrated during the season of Epiphany for illuminating the spiritual experience of epiphany for Christians.

The three Synoptic Gospels record Jesus's baptism with almost identical words. As Jesus came up out of the water, the heavens opened and the Spirit descended like a dove and a voice proclaimed, "This is my beloved Son, with whom I am well pleased" (Matthew 3:16–17; Mark 1:1–10; Luke 3:21–22). Whether everyone in the crowd heard and understood the message of the voice from heaven or whether only John the Baptist and Jesus heard it and understood it or whether only Jesus alone heard and understood it is not made explicit. In John's

Gospel a similar voice from heaven is understood only by Jesus, and the crowd perceives it as thunder (John 12:28–29). In Jesus's baptism the vision of God precedes the expression of identity, but because Jesus was God and knew his own identity, the usual order of self-identity and then encounter with deity is reversed.

The sacrament of baptism is crucial for an understanding of the particularly Christian meaning of epiphany. Because Christian baptism is ordinarily administered to infants in most branches of the Church, it does not usually involve an "experience" in the sense of an event that is understood by the recipient at the time that it occurs. It is important to remember that an epiphany is not always experienced emotionally and rationally and that the event may be interpreted and understood and filled out in meaning later, perhaps over and over again, as it is recalled or even recounted to a person by other people. It is also important to note that an epiphany is not (or at least not just) a theophany. While many epiphanies do include an experience of emotionally or mentally perceived divine mystery as an important element, most baptisms, which are the prototypical Christian epiphanies, do not. While baptism, like all epiphanies, involves an encounter with deity, the meaning of that encounter may not be understood by the recipient at the time. The initial aspect of baptism, like the initial element of all epiphanies, is the endowment of one's true identity. The culminating aspect of baptism, also like that of all epiphanies, is the encounter with a divine presence. In the case of baptism, that divine presence comes in the reception of grace, the gift of God's love and power. (Besides bestowing Christian identity and encountering Christ in the sacrament of baptism, there are also assurances in baptism of being incorporated into Christ, which will be the focus of a following chapter titled "Resurrection.")

For most of those who are baptized as infants, their baptism may be their first encounter with Christ, who for Christians is the truest and ultimate epiphany (manifestation) of God on earth. Even though those baptized may not understand their meeting with Christ, those around them, their families and friends and fellow church members, do know that they are being introduced to Christ and do acknowledge that God's presence in Christ is being incorporated in them. Later the event of their baptism will be related and interpreted to them, much as the story of being held as babies by a president or a prince would be told to them, although an encounter with a president or a prince would have much less importance.

In Christian baptism the infant child is given a name as the sacrament is administered. In older versions of *The Book of Common Prayer* it was implied that the child had no name until baptized.[9] With the name, however, a new and fuller identity is bestowed. A person's emerging true self is revealed.

The nature of the identity given in baptism is expressed succinctly in the chrismation sentence of the Episcopal liturgy, when a person is "marked as Christ's own forever."[10] The prototypical Christian epiphany of baptism bestows on a person the basic identity as one who belongs to Christ and who is raised in Christ to "the new life of grace."[11] Augustine argued vehemently that the "seal" or "mark" of Christian identity given in baptism is permanent and unrepeatable, even when it is received in an unworthy manner by those who believe or behave in ways contrary to orthodox Christian faith or when the officiant may believe or behave in ways contrary to orthodox Christian faith.[12]

The remainder of the newly baptized person's life will entail working out that new identity and discerning what it means to be to be marked as Christ's own forever and raised to the new life of grace.

The Rev. James McReynolds, who tutored and accompanied groups in Russia studying its Orthodox Church, often told the story of Misha, one of the local guides frequently assigned to them. Misha was born during the years of the Soviet Union to strictly doctrinaire Marxist parents, but a babushka slipped him out of his home as an infant and took him to a priest to be baptized. When working with groups of American Christians, Misha would often joke about "being a Christian, too," and tell his story, but he would usually ask, perhaps only half-joking, at the end of his account, "Do you think it makes any difference?" Some of the American Christian pilgrims, speaking out of their sacramental theology, would tell him that his baptism surely did make a difference. He was "marked" as a Christian even if he never chose to activate the divine grace that had been implanted in him. In time, perhaps partly as a result of the American Christians' affirmations, Misha did accept his baptism and expressed his faith openly and actively.

Misha's story is more dramatic than the life journeys that most Christians make following their baptisms, but it may serve as a parable for the way all those who are "marked as Christ's own forever" in the sacrament of baptism must "work out their salvation with fear and trembling" (Philippians 2:12).

The rest of this book will endeavor to make a few suggestions about how that identity is discovered and how the new life of grace plays out. The identity given in baptism means that belonging to Christ takes precedence over all other identities and has priority over all other epiphanies. Moreover, for Christians all other identities and all other epiphanies will be interpreted and understood through the lens of the identity bestowed in the epiphany of baptism.

Epiphanies may happen at the beginning of a human life and throughout a human life, after baptism and before baptism, especially for those who are baptized as adults when evangelized in advanced years or in those branches of the Church that practice "believers' baptism." Epiphanies may arise in a moment of awe elicited by the beauty or even by the powerful terror of the natural world. Epiphanies may occur when wrestling with moral dilemmas or in meeting people of great wisdom and sanctity, whose lives point to an ultimate truth and holiness beyond themselves and their humanity. Epiphanies may also come upon people suddenly and without warning during ordinary and everyday routines. Epiphanies may also be bestowed at the end of a life.

Another story of an archetypal epiphany in the Bible is the martyrdom of Stephen recorded in the Acts of the Apostles. As he was dying Stephen "gazed into heaven and saw the glory of God and Jesus standing at the right hand of God" (Acts 7:55), a vision that echoes the promise that Jesus made to Nathanael at his epiphany during their first meeting at the beginning of his apostolic vocation.

In baptism as in all epiphanies a person is given an identity and glimpses God's presence in a moment of meeting. Other epiphanies, other clarifications of one's identity and further encounters with a divine presence may (and should and usually do) follow as weeks and months and years go by. Epiphanies, even a succession of epiphanies that add depth and clarity to an understanding of one's self identity and the nature of God, are important elements of faith, but they are not the only elements of faith. Knowing God must be completed by loving God and serving God and being joined to God. Epiphanies are just the first steps in a spiritual journey that continues in being transformed by God and sharing in the life of God and participating in the work of God.

Although there is a kind of progression from epiphany to trans-figuration to resurrection to ascension, as those terms are used here, they are not always sequential, and the experiences of epiphany do not stop when a spiritual journey moves into these other realms of faith. Quite the contrary—as Christians are transformed by God and share in the life of God and participate in the work of God, their spiritual experiences of self-awareness and divine presence are thereby enhanced, and they continue to have even fuller epiphanies that expand their self-understanding and deepen their sense of God's grace.

Notes

1   II Thessalonians 2:8; I Timothy 6:14; II Timothy 4:1, 8–9; Titus 2:13. See also Titus 2:11 and 3:4 for the verb form of the word. The verb form is also found in Luke 1:79, where Zechariah prophesies that his son, John the Baptist, will "*bring light* to those who sit in darkness." Hebrews 9:24 uses the verb form to speak of Christ's *appearing* in the presence of God on our behalf. Matthew 27:53 uses the verb to speak of the dead coming out of their graves after Jesus's resurrection and *appearing* to many people. In Romans 10:30 Paul quotes Isaiah using the verb form to affirm God as saying "I *have shown* myself to those who did not ask for me." The words italicized for emphasis could all be used as definitions of epiphany.

2   Once again I remind the reader that this is a personal testimony. I make

no claim nor offer any evidence that this observation is a scholarly position.

3   Mark 1:34 and 3:11–12, compare Matthew 12:16 and Luke 4:41. This contrast between Mark and John should not be overemphasized so as to include all three Synoptic Gospels. Matthew especially records Jesus's rant against the "blindness" of the religious leaders of his time (see Matthew 23:16–23), although in Matthew blindness is more often a metaphor for burdensome and inappropriate religious practices, while in John's Gospel blindness is a metaphor for the spiritual failure to discern Christ's origin in God (see John 9:35–41).

4   Luke also details Jesus's commendation of Samaritans, including especially his parable of the "Good Samaritan." See Luke 9:51–54, 10:29–37, and 17:11–19. The Samaritans were a colony of people who remained in the area during the Babylonian exile and intermarried with non-Jews imported there from Babylon and elsewhere and then adopted some of their customs and religious practices. They continued to pay allegiance to the Temple in Jerusalem, but when their offers to help with the rebuilding of the Temple were rejected during the puritanical regime of Ezra and Nehemiah, relationships between Judea and Samaria became increasingly hostile. Eventually Samaritans erected their own temple on Mt. Gerizim near the partriarchal religious site of Shechem and claimed that the temple in David's city was a late, illegitimate accretion to the faith. They revered only the Torah and dismissed the prophetic books of the Hebrew scriptures. By the time of Jesus, Samaritans were regarded in Judea and Galilee as half-pagan, impure, and not truly Jewish. See "Samaritans," *Harper's Bible Dictionary*, Harper and Brothers, sixth edition, 1959, pp. 639–640; and D. J Wiseman, "Samaritans," *The New Bible Dictionary*, Inter-Varsity Press, 1962, pp. 1131–1132.

5   *Oxford English Dictionary of the Christian Church*, pp. 457–458.

6   Paul refers to his epiphany on the Damascus Road in I Corinthians 15:8 and Galatians 1:15, but only Luke supplies the detailed narrative in Acts.

7   "Against Julian," chapter seven in Matthew A. Schumacher's translation, *Fathers of the Church*, 1957, p. 330. See also "On Baptism," chapter eight, Denis Kavangh, translator, *St. Augustine's Commentary of the Lord's Supper with Seventeen Related Sermons*, Fathers of the Church, 1951, p. 336. In the sermon Augustine refers to "the circumcision of the flesh" as a "seal," which is an important concept in his theology of baptism, discussed below.

8   "Quicunque Vult," *The Book of Common Prayer*, p. 865.

9   *The Book of Common Prayer*, The Seabury Press, 1928, p. 279.

10 *The Book of Common Prayer* (1977), p. 308.

11 Ibid.

12 Augustine engaged in a long controversy with the Donatists, who insisted on rebaptism if the sacrament had been performed by an unworthy priest or given to an unworthy candidate or one who later lapsed and denied and then returned to the Christian faith. He often used the analogy of a soldier who deserted and returned to the army but was still "marked as a soldier of the king" whose "character" would not ". . . be repeated which had once been sealed." Augustine apparently uses "character" much as I use "identity" to describe an authentic self in a particular context, such as a soldier in the army or a baptized Christian in the Church or in modern times a physician or a lawyer certified by a professional board. In the citation above Augustine wrote about those who had lapsed from faith and then returned, but he used the same analogy in writing about heretics. See "The Creed," chapter eight, translated by Marie Liguori, *Writings of St. Augustine*, Vol. 15, The Catholic University of America Press, 1955, p. 306. For a summary of Donatism see *The Oxford English Dictionary of the Christian Church*, p. 415.

Transfiguration

"All of us, with unveiled faces, seeing the glory of the Lord as though reflected in a mirror, are being 'transformed' ["metamorphoo" in Greek] into the same image from one degree of glory to another; for this comes from the Lord, the Spirit." — II CORINTHIANS 3:18

Although this section is titled "Transfiguration" to conform to the familiar name of the event in Jesus's life that is remembered on a feast day in liturgical churches, the meditations about the process in Christians' lives on the following pages would probably be better described as "transformation." The Greek word "metamorphoo" is rarely used in the New Testament, twice for the event when Jesus's face and garments were perceived as dazzling white on the mountain-top and twice by Paul—in the quotation above and in Romans 12:2. In all cases it employs the passive voice, but in both older and newer translations of the Bible the event in Jesus's life is rendered in English as "transfigured" and as "transformed" in the passages from Paul's letters.[1] In this chapter the term "transfigured" will always be used to identify the event on the mountaintop when Jesus's appearance became radiant. "Transformation" and "transfiguration" will both be used with the same intended meaning to refer to the Christian's journey of faith, but the use of "transformation" will predominate.

The event of Jesus's transfiguration on the mountaintop provides a bridge from the Christian experience of epiphany to the Christian experience of transfiguration. When Jesus was baptized by John in the Jordan River, a voice from heaven proclaimed: "You are my beloved son, with whom I am well pleased" (Matthew 3:17; Mark 1:11; Luke 3:22), and on the mountaintop in the midst of his ministry with his disciples, the voice from heaven proclaimed to Peter, James, and John, "This is my beloved son, listen to him!" As noted in the previous chapter, it is ambiguous whether the heavenly voice at Jesus's baptism was understood only by him or also by John the Baptist and others nearby. At the transfiguration the proclamation was specifically given for the benefit and understanding of the three disciple leaders.[2] The event is also remembered in the letter of II Peter, when Peter not only recalls the voice proclaiming, "This is my beloved Son . . ." but also affirms that "we ourselves heard this voice from heaven, while we were with him on the holy mountain" (1:17–18).

Whatever the actual change in the appearance of Jesus may have been is beyond the scope of this book and probably beyond the ken of human understanding, but in this chapter the attention will be focused on the experience of Peter, James, and John. For them the transfiguration of Jesus was an epiphany. Since it happened toward the end of their time with Jesus before his death, it was an epiphany within their process of being transformed. Although they may not have fully understood that Jesus was God incarnate until after the resurrection, the event of the transfiguration was an event in their lives when they more nearly appreciated Jesus's divinity than they had previously been able to understand.

A part of spiritual transformation is a succession of epiphanies, which lead progressively to greater and greater appreciation of a divine presence. Epiphanies provide only a part of transformation, however, and what Jesus had taught Peter and James and John, what they had observed and witnessed, what they had meditated upon, all contributed to the spiritual changes in them that could be described as their own transformation, which reached a moment of climax in witnessing Jesus's transfiguration.

An epiphany is almost by definition initiated and completely directed by God. Human beings cannot decide to have epiphanies and manufacture those experiences for themselves. Although spiritual disciplines and openness may prepare for an epiphany, it often comes about suddenly, unexpectedly, surprisingly. Even in the sacrament of baptism God's unmerited grace dominates and initiates the encounter with Christ.

God is also the major actor in the process of spiritual transformation. God transforms people by grace. People do not transform themselves. The role of human faith is larger, however, in the spiritual process of being transfigured by God. The disciplines of prayer and meditation, a cultivated attitude of spiritual openness, study of scripture, pondering the meaning of successive epiphanies, and sharing the stories and fellowship of others who have experienced God's presence all prepare both for new and more meaningful epiphanies and also for other aspects of companionship with God. Although people are transfigured by the action of God in their lives, their human intellects and emotions and wills play roles in their receptiveness to becoming transformed.

The involvement of the body is another facet of the process of transformation. In the letter to the Romans when Paul writes about how we are transformed (transfigured), he enjoins his readers to present their bodies as living sacrifices and not to be "conformed to this world, but be transformed by the renewing of your minds, so that you may discern what is the good and acceptable and perfect will of God" (Romans 12:1–2). While the epitome of a Christian epiphany brings a recognition of God in the incarnated Christ, the epitome of Christian transfiguration involves the transformation of the whole person, often including the physical body, which of course leads to the meditations in the next chapter when Christ's resurrection is joined to the resurrection of his followers.

A brief synopsis of the lives of several giants of faith may offer clues about the process of transfiguration. The life of Moses provides the greatest detail that is recorded in the Hebrew scriptures about the process of spiritual transformation over years and decades, and the apostles Peter and Paul offer the fullest account of spiritual transformation in the New Testament.

Moses's outrage at the cruelty of an overseer and his identification with the Hebrew people reflect the first phase of his transformation recorded in the Bible. When he slew one of the overseers and fled to

Media, another stage of the process of his transformation became evident in his choosing the ancestry of his birth over the training and enculturation of his Egyptian adoption, thus illustrating the mystery of the combination of human choice and will with divine providence (Exodus 2:11–15). The tutelage in Media by his father-in-law Jethro gave Moses a religious understanding of God that prepared him for his archetypal epiphany at the burning bush (Exodus 3). Not only his education in the Egyptian court and his mentoring by Jethro but also his personality shaped Moses's style of leadership (Exodus 18). His humility and recognition of his limitations, such as his inability to speak in public, resulted in sharing leadership first with his brother and sister, Aaron and Miriam, and later with seventy elders chosen to assist him in governing (Numbers 11:11–25; Exodus 4 and 18).

Moses's culminating epiphanies—when he met God on Sinai, which probably served as models for the accounts by the gospel writers of Jesus's transfiguration—resulted in an ethical constitution, the Ten Commandments, which was then elaborated into a complex set of hundreds of laws for religious, civic, and social behavior. In his encounters with God, Moses often pleaded for the needs and desires of the Hebrew people as well as for his own needs and desires, so that the divine disposition and the human involvement are both evident in the process of his transformation (Exodus 20, 31, 32, 34 and 37 and the books of Numbers and Leviticus). The appearance of Moses like that of Jesus (or one could say that of Jesus like that of Moses) was so altered by his epiphanies in his encounters with God that his countenance shown in ways that startled and amazed his followers, much as Jesus's three disciples responded to his transfiguration (Exodus 34:29–30). Moses's vision of the promised land from Mt. Nebo just before his death might be the final epiphany of his transfiguration (Deuteronomy 34) and can offer a background for the meditation on the resurrection which will follow in the next chapter.

The story of Moses offers a fuller account than any other in the Bible about the process of transformation over many decades of a lifetime and demonstrates the interaction between divine action and human response. His biography shows how a life is transformed during seemingly mundane happenstances in daily activities, which prove to be providential in retrospect. It tells about successions of epiphanies and the struggles to integrate them into actual practice in worldly affairs alongside the perdurability of human personality traits that are shaped by spiritual encounters.

The biographies of Peter and Paul suffer in comparison to the story of Moses from fewer details over a shorter span of time, but they benefit from their encounters with God in Christ, which for Christians are the ultimate experiences that transform them. Peter's epiphanies can be itemized by the sequence of occasions when he heard Christ say "follow me" over the course of his lifetime. His first encounter with Jesus recounted by Matthew and Mark was the call to fish for people (Matthew 4:18–22; Mark 1:16–20, compare John 1:40–43). The second time that Jesus told Peter to "follow me" occurs after Peter's testimony that Jesus was the Christ, the son of the living God, at Caesarea Philippi, when Jesus told Peter and other disciples to follow him even to the cross by denying themselves (Matthew 16:13–26; Mark 8:27–38; Luke 9:18–26). Sometime after he had witnessed Jesus's transfiguration Peter spoke in the third instance of leaving everything to follow Jesus and was promised a reward of eternal life (Matthew 19:27–29; Mark 10:28–30; Luke 18:28–30). In the fourth example Peter followed Jesus in fear and cowardice at a distance to the house of Caiaphas where he denied Jesus three times after vowing never to leave him (Matthew 2:34, 58, 69–75; Mark 14:29, 54, 66–72; Luke 22:34, 54, 56–62; John 13:26–27 and 18:15, 17, 25–27).[3] The account of Peter following another disciple into the tomb seeking Jesus's body and finding it empty may be reckoned as the fifth record of his following, although it is rather different from the others in lacking an audible vocal call from the Lord (John 20:19). After Peter was asked three times by the Risen Christ if he loved him, Peter was called for a sixth and final time to "follow me" (John 21:15–19).

In the midst of these calls for Peter to follow Christ, he had seen others who followed Jesus or were called to do so: a disciple who wanted to delay in order to bury his father and is told to put no priority ahead of God's summons (Matthew 8:21–22; Luke 9:59–60); Matthew (Levi) who was called to be a disciple at his tax booth (Matthew 9:9; Mark 2:14; Luke 5:27–28); perhaps two blind men, who sought to be healed (Matthew 9:27–31; 20:34); and numerous times when great crowds followed Jesus (among them, Matthew 4:25; 8:10; 12:15; 14:13; 19:2; 20:29; 21:9: 27:55; Mark 3:7; 6:33; 10:1, 46; 11:18; 15:40–41; Luke 7:9; 6:17; 9:11; 19:37).

Peter has also heard Jesus teach about the importance of following him—"Whoever does not take up his cross and follow me is not worthy of me" (Matthew 10:38); "whoever serves me must follow me, and wherever I am, there will my servant be also" (John 8:12); "whoever follows me will never walk in darkness but will have the light of life" (John 8:12); ". . . the sheep follow [the good shepherd] because they know his voice; he calls his own sheep by name and leads them out" (John 10:4–5).

Through all of these times that Peter had heard and heeded or neglected Jesus's call to "follow me," he was being transformed. After each call to "follow me," Peter was led to a successively deeper and fuller understanding and was also transfigured to be the man God intended and Christ beckoned him to be. His human nature wrestled with the divine presence in Jesus. He failed and succeeded. He was overwhelmed, and he overcame. He lost his vision of Christ and saw God revealed in Jesus. Braggadocio, humility, cowardice, bravery, obtuseness, insight, spontaneity, and reluctance are all observed in Peter. His human qualities were transfigured over time by his involvement with God in Christ.

One aspect of transfiguration involves the prediction and promise of what a person will become in the future, even before the transformation has been fully realized. When Jesus gave the nickname "Peter" to Simon, making a pun on the word "rock" (*petra*), the disciple was far from being the solid unwavering apostle who could later truly be called a rock of faith (Matthew 16:18).[4]

A climactic point in the sequence of the calls to "follow me" was reached when the Risen Christ addressed Peter on the lakeshore, but it is important to note that in the progressive transfiguration of Peter there is not a decisive break or distinction between the calls to "follow me" by Jesus before his death and the final call to "follow me" by Christ after the resurrection. Although the letter of I Peter may not have been actually penned by the Apostle Peter, it surely reflects his transformation in its characterization of "a witness of the sufferings of Christ as well as one who shares the glory to be revealed" (5:1).

By the time Peter preached the sermon on the first Christian Pentecost, the traditional birth of the Church (Acts 2:14–26), it might be assumed that his transformation was completed. Not only was Peter the featured spokesman and evangelist in the early church, but along with John he also continued the healing ministry of Jesus. Sick people were even carried into the streets and placed in a position that allowed the shadows of Peter and John to fall over them in the hope of their being cured (Acts 5:15). Soon afterward Peter was imprisoned and then miraculously released from jail, and the process of his transfiguration continued (Acts 4 and 12). There was still a significant epiphany in store for Peter, however, when he "fell into a trance and saw the heavens opened and something like a sheet coming down" (Acts 10:11). Peter was commanded to eat creatures that were regarded by pious Jews as unclean. The next day Peter met the Roman centurion Cornelius and understood that the meaning of his vision was God's desire to include Gentiles in the Church (Acts 10:30–48). Peter later worked out more details for the instrumentality of including Gentile believers as he engaged in debates and conflicts with Paul.

The final great epiphany in the process of Peter's transfiguration is a reminder that spiritual transformation continues throughout the lifetime of a religious pilgrim. Although the day after his vision Peter began to understand the meaning of his epiphany concerning the inclusion of Gentile believers, working out its implementations and consequences required months and years. Transfiguration involves more than a succession of epiphanies, however dramatic and significant they may be. The ways they are interpreted and incorporated into behavior are also germane to the fullness of spiritual transformation.

Although Luke supplies much biographical material about Paul's life in the Acts of the Apostles, the comparison of details to the accounts about Peter and Moses may seem limited. Yet, Paul almost uniquely in the New Testament writes autobiographically and shares his personal theology in his letters, which make up about a quarter of the words in the New Testament.

More attention will be given to Paul's personal theology in the next section of this book titled "Resurrection," but in the first chapter of his letter to the Galatians Paul recounts some of the events of his spiritual pilgrimage, both before and immediately after his epiphany on the Damascus Road when the Risen Christ appeared to him. He does not apologize for his attacks on Jesus's followers before his epiphany nor for his advancement as a young man in the study of Judaism. The process of transfiguration for Paul is forward looking, not backward looking. He writes about his retreat for a time in Arabia in order to ponder and meditate on his experience, and he also recalls his visit to Jerusalem three years later to confer with Peter and Jesus's brother James in order to understand his epiphany in the context of other believers' experiences and knowledge. Then he refers to another long period of reflection while living in Syria as he began working out the call to his apostleship on behalf of the Gentiles that he had first experienced on the Damascus Road.

In the second chapter of this same letter to the Galatians Paul wrote about another epiphany when it was revealed to him that Gentile believers should not have to observe the ritual practices of the Jews, especially not have to be circumcised or eat kosher foods in order to be full participants in the Church. It was this later epiphany that brought Paul into debate and conflict with Peter, as both of them had to work through the implications of their epiphanies. Often transfiguration involves other people who help to shape and bring to light the daily actions and responses that are involved in the process of being transformed.

Paul also wrote in his correspondence with the church in Corinth about yet another ecstatic epiphany, some six years after his experience of the Risen Christ on the Damascus Road (II Corinthians 12:1–2). However indelibly that experience was impressed on his memory, he emphasized the greater importance of struggling with his vocation in shepherding the Gentile believers in the process of his spiritual transformation. A fuller account of how Paul struggled with his own human weakness and confronted antagonism in establishing the Gentile churches will be surveyed in the next chapter, as those experiences led Paul to affirm his hope and belief of incorporation into Christ.

Luke related Paul's dream about a man in Macedonia calling him to come and help them (Acts 16:9–10). Although Paul had desired to go farther into Asia (Minor), Luke wrote cryptically that the Holy Spirit forbade him. Thus Paul turned westward and perhaps the future territory of Christendom was thereby altered. Paul's biography illustrates probably more clearly than any other biblical narrative how greatly vocation and transformation are intertwined and how they are both impelled forward by successive epiphanies.

In Luke's account of Paul's travels to the churches with largely Gentile members, he describes the conflicts Paul experienced not only with congregations, which Paul describes in greater detail in his letters, but also with other leaders—Peter, mentioned above, and Barnabas, with whom Paul argued about their aide, John Mark (Acts 15:36–41). Luke also describes the hardships and perils that Paul endured, which Paul summarizes in a letter to Corinth: "Five times I have received from the Jews the forty lashes minus one. Three times I was beaten with rods. Once I received a stoning. Three times I was shipwrecked; for a night and a day I was adrift at sea . . ." (II Corinthians 11:24–27). All of these experiences—ecstatic epiphanies, persecutions, conflicts, even ecclesiastical administration—contributed to the transfiguration of Paul that culminated in his affirmation of union with the Risen Christ, as the transformed life of faith reached its consummation in resurrection.

A brief survey of the lives of Francis of Assisi and the Buddha reflects many of the same characteristics of development found in the transfigurations of biblical characters. After war, imprisonment, and illness Francis had an epiphany that led him to devote himself to prayer and service to the poor. Later he swapped his clothing with a beggar during a pilgrimage to Rome and stripped himself naked in an argument with his father about his vocational intentions. While he was ministering to lepers and rebuilding the ruined church of San Damiano, he experienced another epiphany in a vision of Christ calling Francis to leave everything and follow him. Later in one of the most dramatic examples of how the physical body is involved in spiritual transformation, Francis's hands were literally transfigured with marks of crucifixion.[5]

Followers flocked to the Buddha after his epiphany, which came to be called an enlightenment, in a way similar to how Francis was surrounded by people attracted to him. Both Francis and the Buddha founded lasting movements that have endured and flourished over the centuries, perhaps despite their original intentions and designs. Again paralleling some of the experiences of the young Francis, the encounters with old age, disease, and death by the young Siddhartha Gautama prompted him to engage in a life of asceticism and self-mortification. His great epiphany occurred several years later when he was enlightened while sitting under a Bo tree and so was designated the Buddha (the enlightened one). Although the teachings of the Buddha like those of the Christ are complex and profound, they both enjoy clear and simple statements, which in Buddhism include the Four Noble Truths and the Eightfold Path.[6]

The life of the Buddha and the practice of Buddhism have always seemed to me the closest non-biblical parallels to the life of Christ and Christianity except for the stories of the saints in church history. Remarkable similarities may be observed between Francis's transfiguration and Gautama's enlightenment and in their subsequent experiences and even in the outcomes of their influence on their followers. Yet, as the Christian pilgrimage continues in the descriptions that follow in the chapters titled "Resurrection" and "Ascension," correlations between the Christian experiences and those of other religions and philosophies will be more difficult to discern (which is not to say that they do not exist). The epiphanies that would seem to be a common phenomenon of being human become more particularized and uniquely shaped as they lead in Christian faith to sharing the life and work of God. Others may speak meaningfully about their participaton in these experiences, but Christians can testify to them only by their relationship to Jesus Christ.

The ultimate result of a fully transfigured life, one that knows and obeys God completely, is manifested in Jesus, just as the totally enlightened one is modeled in the Buddha, but Christians do not have as clear and simple a summary as the Four Noble Truths and the Eightfold Path. Perhaps the closest statement that briefly describes what the transformed Christian life involves is found in I John: "Beloved, let us love one another, because love is from God; everyone who loves is born of God and knows God. Whoever does not love does not know God, for God is love. God's love was revealed among us in this way: God sent his only Son into the world so that we might live through him" (4:7–9).

The sacramental rites of unction and the reconciliation of a penitent do not correspond as closely to transfiguration as does baptism to epiphany nor as does communion to resurrection, but rather they provide examples of some events in the progressive journey of being transformed into the image of Christ. In the brief biographical sketches above the conditions of illness and death in the experiences of Francis and the Buddha and the experiences of shame, denial, regret and conflict in the experiences of Peter and Paul might have led them, if they had all lived and participated in a liturgical church of a later era, to seek out the sacramental rites of unction and the reconciliation of a penitent.

It is not so much the events and experiences which bring people to request those sacramental actions that represent transfigured lives but rather the result and efficaciousness of the rites that exemplify their transformative potential. Some healing of the physical body often follows unction. As noted at several junctures above, the physical body is often involved in transfiguration. The principal effect of unction, however, is focused on moving toward an integrated wholeness of the person, in which the spiritual components dominate. A distinction can be drawn between being healed and being cured. (A similar distinction will be made in the next chapter between resurrection and resuscitation.) Although some people may experience a degree of being physically cured following unction, almost all will find a movement within themselves toward a healing often manifested in peace, joy, and calm assurance and acceptance of their lives and circumstances, all of which are signs of their transformation.

In non-liturgical churches the effects of prayer for the sick may demonstrate some of the same outcomes, although they may not be as focused and immediate as the signs of transfiguration associated with sacramental unction. The letter of James gives the instruction and the hopeful outcome for the healing of the sick: "Are any among you sick? They should call for the elders of the church and have them pray over them, anointing them with oil in the name of the Lord. The prayer of faith will save the sick, and the Lord will raise them up; and anyone who has committed sins will be forgiven" (5:14–15).

As James continues, the background for the sacramental rite of the reconciliation of a penitent is enunciated: "Therefore confess your sins to one another, so that you may be healed. The prayer of the righteous is powerful and effective" (5:16).

It is evident that unction and the reconciliation of a penitent, which is familiarly called "confession," are closely associated, both in their intention and in their outcome. Echoing the words of James a rubric (or direction) for the reconciliation of a penitent in *The Book of Common Prayer* states that the rite "is exercised through the care each Christian has for others . . ."[7] Unlike other sacramental rites (with the exception of emergency baptism, which should be formalized later by an ordained person), provision is made for any Christian person, lay or ordained, to hear the confession of another. In the Celtic church, out of which the sacrament of confession arose and was refined, Christians were paired as *anam caras*, or soul friends, who would hear each others' confessions and offered spiritual advice, counsel, and direction as witnesses to their mutual continuing transformation in Christ.

In modern liturgical churches, of course, confessions are usually heard by priests in the Episcopal Church and always by priests in the Roman Catholic Church. In my own ministry of more than four decades in the Episcopal Church I have heard scores of confessions and often witnessed the transfiguration of people's lives sometimes in the very moments after the sacramental action but more often in the days and weeks immediately following. It is important to maintain absolute confidentiality about what is said during a confession, so that the subject of a particular confession should not usually be revealed even anonymously. On several occasions, however, people who had not received communion for a long time, in one case for a number of years, felt freed to take the sacrament on the Sunday following their confession. Their expressions of joy and delight radiated on their faces after the service. Often the spiritual problem confessed did not seem to me a very grave sin, but somehow it was perceived by them as an obstacle to God's grace, as a betrayal of a loved one, or as a personal deception, that prevented the reception of the Eucharist.

In addition to the sacraments, the involvement of the physical body in the process of spiritual transformation is symbolized by the movement of bodies during worship in liturgical churches. Prayer, praise, contrition, and other spiritual responses are expressed by bowing, standing, kneeling, genuflecting, and making the sign of the cross.[8] A similar kind of expression of the body in worship can be observed in Pentecostal churches, although the gestures may be different from those of liturgical churches and include raising hands into the air, swaying, and even falling to the ground.

There were also other occasions numbered in the hundreds or even the thousands, when I saw the evidence of transfiguration in events that were not related to defined sacramental rites or even to formalized worship but might be legitimately called sacramental in nature. People who endured a lingering illness, those who remained faithful over months and years to an errant spouse or child, those who grieved about a terrible loss, all provided the contexts for spiritual transformations that I witnessed, often unknown to others—the confidence of the clergy is one of the great privileges of an ordained ministry. Not all transfigurations took place in sorrowful circumstances, however, and especially during my longest tenure of seventeen years in one parish, I observed the gradual spiritual growth of people as they overcame problems and prevailed victorious over their sins through prayer and worship.

Some of the most dramatic and visible occasions of transfiguration involved people's participation in the various twelve step programs that originated from Alcoholics Anonymous. The transformation of the physical body as well as the spiritual transfiguration of the whole person became palpable in people who sincerely and completely submitted themselves to that healing process. Their visible transfiguration not only in the health of their physical bodies but also in their daily behavior sometimes appeared miraculous. They were perhaps the closest equivalents in my own observation to the many accounts of Jesus's healing recorded in the Gospels. (In the introduction I wrote that the four short stories in the back of this book do not each correspond to particular chapters of theological reflection, but the second short story might be read especially in conjunction with this chapter, although it may have motifs that touch the other chapters as well.)

Although AA is spiritually based and was initiated by people who were practicing Christians, its practice does not require a commitment to Christianity nor to any specific religious profession. Like Buddhists the people involved in twelve step programs may be transformed through practices outside the Christian faith, but these transformations also resemble Christian transfiguration.

My observations about twelve step programs illustrate how epiphanies and transfigurations may be common to people in their shared humanity, although they may be given a particular shape in Christianity. Spiritual transformation often bears similar characteristics and parallel stages of development across lines of religion or even humanist philosophies. As mentioned above, however, resurrection and ascension, as those terms are used in the typology of this book, bring the spiritual pilgrim into realms more specifically associated with Jesus Christ and unique to the Christian faith.

Notes

1   Matthew 17:2 and Mark 9:2 use *metamorphoo* in the narrative of Jesus's transfiguration; Luke's description of Jesus's transfiguration, which parallels the descriptions of Matthew and Mark, does not use the word itself. The NRSV, RSV, KJV all translate *metamorphoo*, from which the English word metamorphosis is derived, as "transfigured" in Matthew and Mark. In the other two places where *metamorphoo* is used in the New Testament, the quotation from II Corinthians at the head of this chapter is translated as "transformed" in the NRSV and as changed in the RSV and KJV. In the quotation from Romans 12:2, which will be discussed below, it is translated as "transformed" by the NRSV, RSV, and KJV. A completely different word, *metaschematizo*, in II Corinthians 11:13–15, where Paul writes about the deception by false apostles, is translated as "transfigured" by the KJV but more aptly rendered as "disguised" by the NRSV and RSV. That same word, *metaschematizo*, is translated as "transformed" in Philippians 3:21 in the NRSV and changed in the RSV and KJV; but it means "completely changed in form" and will be discussed below in the chapter titled "Resurrection." In I Corinthians 4:6 Paul uses *metashematizo* in a phrase which is a figure of speech: "I have given this teaching of mine 'the form of' an exposition concerning Apollos and myself." See W. F. Arndt and F. W. Gingrich, *A Greek-English Lexicon of the New Testament and Other Early Christian Literature*, The University of Chicago Press, 1957, p. 515.

2   Matthew has "This is my beloved son" in the narrative of both events. Mark and Luke distinguish more explicitly between the voice addressing Jesus, recording "This is my beloved son" at the transfiguration and "You are my beloved son" at his baptism, but all three Synoptic Gospels add the words from heaven to the transfiguration account, which are not found in the account of Jesus's baptism, "Listen to him!"

3   This is one of the remarkable incidents that is recalled but not "copied" in exact words in all four Gospels, which points both to its authority and to its importance in the memory of early Christians.

4   Although the pun is possible in the Greek language of the Gospel writers, (*Petra* and *petros*), a pun is also possible in the Aramaic, which Jesus probably spoke, between *Kepha* and *kepha*. See Howard Clark Kee, "The Gospel According to Matthew" in *The Interpreters' One Volume Commentary on the Bible*, Abingdon Press, 1971, p. 629.

5   *Oxford English Dictionary of the Christian Church*, pp. 520–521.

6   The brief synopsis of the life of the Buddha is drawn from my memory
    and study over previous years, and I have no specific references to cite.

7   *The Book of Common Prayer*, p. 446.

8   For a fuller reflection see Scott Walters, "Bodies at worship," *The Christian
    Century*, September 22, 2009, vol. 126, no. 19, p. 13.

Resurrection

"If the Spirit of him who raised Jesus from the dead dwells in you, he who raised Christ from the dead will give life to your mortal bodies also through his Spirit that dwells in you." — ROMANS 8:11

Because many notions of "life after death" are associated with the idea of resurrection in people's minds today, it is necessary to begin by noting what is not meant by resurrection here. It is not an immortal soul, which separates from the flesh at the time of death, as the ancient Greeks and probably most modern American have believed. Nor is it the resuscitation of the flesh, although the body is involved, as anticipated in the previous chapter where it was noted that the body is often affected by transfiguration. In fact completely different words are used in the New Testament for resuscitation (*egeiro*) in such miracles as the raising of Lazarus and Jairus's daughter, Tabitha, and for the resurrection (*anatasis*) of Jesus (Mark 5:21–24, 35–42; John 11:11–44).

Perhaps even thornier questions arise in considering the various biblical ideas of resurrection in successive eras of Hebrew, Christian, and Jewish history. Probably those who believed in resurrection at the time of Jesus put their emphasis on an event at the end of history. In some periods of Hebrew history a greater emphasis was placed on the restoration of the whole people of Israel than on the resurrection of individual people.[1] Those beliefs will be considered both in the discussion of the hope for resurrection in the world to come in this chapter and also in the discussion of what is meant by ascension in the next chapter.

For some Christians an understanding of resurrection is grounded in a belief in the resurrection of Jesus and in the accounts of the appearances of the Risen Christ in the four Gospels. As Paul wrote to the church in Corinth, "... we know that the one who raised the Lord Jesus will raise us also with Jesus, and will bring us with you into his presence" (II Corinthians 4:14). After his resurrection Christ was eventually identified by his followers but not always immediately recognized by them. The first witness at the empty tomb, Mary Magdalene, mistook him for a gardener. Despite tears in her eyes, she would surely have recognized Jesus before his death. She identified him when he called her name, "Mary," and the call to self-awareness is reminiscent of what usually happens in an epiphany (John 20:11–16).

The two travelers on the Emmaus Road, who had known Jesus and one of whom may have been related to him, failed to recognize him until he identified himself as they ate together. (Luke 24:13–35 describes their recognition with an obvious reference to the Eucharist, which will be discussed below.) Thomas, who doubted the resurrection, identified Christ by the mark of the wounds from the cross (John 20:26–29). Other disciples of Jesus also recognized him by seeing the wounds on his risen body (Luke 24:39–40). Thus Christ's risen body was related to the body of his flesh that had been nailed to the cross, but now it could pass through walls and locked doors, appear suddenly and disappear in an instant, and yet consume broiled fish (Luke 24:42–43; cf. John 21:13).

The body of the Risen Christ is obviously different from and yet also related to the body of his flesh that lived before his death on the cross. The two Greek words for flesh (*sarx*) and for body (*soma*) are often used by Paul to distinguish between the physical bodies of our present lives (*sarx*, which may also be *soma*) and other kinds of bodies (which are *soma* but are never *sarx*). In his correspondence with the church in Corinth, Paul uses the analogy of a seed that is planted and the new sprout that is born from it to describe the distinction between Jesus's earthly body (*sarx*) of flesh and his risen body (*soma*) of glory as well as their relationship (I Corinthians 15).

Because a body like that of the Risen Christ cannot be examined with modern empirical methods, the evidence of the paradoxical testimonies of the apostles and family members and friends who saw the Risen Christ within a few days after his resurrection must be relied on. Perhaps it was the foreordained plan of God that Christ's resurrection must be appropriated by faith rather than through scientific explanation.

Although the basis of our hope is found in the resurrection of Jesus, most of the discussion in this chapter focuses on what resurrection means for us today in our present lives and in our hope for the world to come. Our resurrection is not limited to our hope for sharing the life of God in the world to come nor to the perfection of our spiritual transformation by God in our present lives, but resurrection pertains both to our hope for life with God beyond the grave and also to our present lives in the world today.

Paul refers to the Risen Christ as a new creation and the first born of both the original creation as well as the first born of the new creation into whose image we will also finally be transformed (II Corinthians 5:17; Galatians 6:15). The new creation witnessed in the Risen Christ and to be inherited by us is an "image of the invisible God" (Colossians 1:15). This new creation, like the original creation, involves more than discrete individual people and includes also the interrelation of all life, a theme that will be explored further in the next chapter.

Already in the present bodies of flesh, people begin to partake of this new creation through a quality of existence that the New Testament writers most often call eternal life. When Paul and John use the words "eternal life," they usually bear a double reference both to our present existence in this world and to our hope for participation in the world to come. Unlike the popular conception today, however, the references to eternal life in the letters of Paul and John usually emphasize our existence in the present world.

Paul affirmed that those who have received Christ Jesus continue to live their lives in him (Colossians 2:6), and John summarizes the purpose of God's sending his Son into the world, "so that we might live through him" (John 4:19). In the Gospel of John, Jesus says that he came "that they may have life and have it abundantly" (John 10:10). Paul even goes so far as to claim that he no longer lives but that Christ lives in him (Galatians 2:20). The mystery of this indwelling of Christ in us and of us in Christ may be as rationally difficult to comprehend as the nature of Christ's risen body. Albert Schweitzer commented on this indwelling: "The capacity which the elect person acquires through the dying and rising again with Christ is, that the soul-body which constitutes his essence is prepared to give up immediately its union with the fleshly body and enter upon that with the glorified body."[2]

Most religious language relies on analogy, because to explain God fully and precisely in human terms is idolatry. In terms of resurrection, however, analogies are even more distant from the perceived reality than in other religious categories, because we are dealing with areas that cannot be empirically verified. For that reason more than usual caution must be observed in using them, lest they distort the divine meaning toward which they point.

The mystery of our living in Christ and of Christ living in us in the analogy of adoption, often used by Paul, points more closely to the spiritual meaning than does deification or divinization, which nevertheless represent the language used by the Eastern Church.[3] By participating in the death and resurrection of Christ we are enabled to share in the life of God through the sacrificial incarnation of our brother Christ Jesus (Galatians 4:4–5), but we do not become God, and God does not become us.

Epiphany, transfiguration, and resurrection as terms used here typologically are not necessarily sequential or progressive. To be sure there is a certain sense in which we know God in Christ before we are transformed by divine grace and then find a culmination of Christ's indwelling in resurrection. It is also true that God's transfiguring grace begins to work within us before we have a conscious awareness of the divine presence, as was noted in the discussion of the sacrament of baptism in the previous chapter "Epiphany." During our transfiguration throughout the span of our lifetimes, we continue to have epiphanies, which, as described above, are parts of the process of our transformation. Perhaps even more closely related than epiphany and transfiguration, however, are transfiguration and resurrection. Throughout our lives we may be aware at particular moments of how we live in Christ and how Christ lives in us. The Irish hymn of the seventh century beautifully expresses this indwelling as "I ever with thee and thou with me, Lord; . . . thou in me dwelling and I one with thee."[4] Those moments may be described as particular kinds of epiphanies and also as belonging to the process of our transformation. In some ways transfiguration might be thought of as the process of our life in Christ, and resurrection might be considered the product of our life in Christ.

Resurrection might also be understood as the goal of our trans-formation in the world, which in the beliefs of some religions and philosophies may or may not continue beyond our death in the flesh. In terms of Christian faith and hope our transfiguration surely does continue and culminates with risen bodies in the world to come. Paul affirms explicitly that "if Christ has not been raised, your faith is futile . . ." and "if for this life only we have hoped in Christ, we are of all people most to be pitied" (I Corinthians 15:17, 19). And yet, the emphasis in Paul's letters is on the increasing dominance of resurrection in our present lives. He expressed this indwelling to the faithful in the Colossian church by reminding them that "as you have received Christ Jesus the Lord, continue to live your lives [walk] in him" (Colossians 2:6). To the community of faith in Philippi, toward which he arguably expressed his most intimate and vulnerable feelings, Paul wrote, "I want to know Christ and the power of his resurrection . . . Not that I have already obtained this or have already reached the goal . . ." (Phi-lippians 3:1, 12). Paul tells the Christians in Galatia that he anticipates Christ being formed in them (Galatians 4:19), and the Christians in Ephesus are encouraged to ". . . grow up in every way . . . into Christ" (Ephesians 4:15).

Once again the insights of Albert Schweitzer are illuminating re-garding the effect of resurrection in Christians' present earthly lives: "Since in the nature of their corporeity they are now assimilated to Jesus Christ, they become, through His death and resurrection, beings in whom dying and rising again have already begun, although the outward seeming of their natural existence remains unchanged."[5]

Paul's focus on Jesus's crucifixion as the ultimate act of divine grace in Christ caused him to wish to share Christ's suffering and become like him even in his death, so that he might finally attain the resurrection from the dead, but also in this world Paul can affirm that "Christ Jesus has made me his own" (Philippians 3:10–11). Paul believed as the physical body of his flesh became weaker and more fragile leading him toward death that his eternal life became stronger and even more visibly like that of Jesus (II Corinthians 4:10–11, cf. Romans 8:10). Thus the affirmations of resurrection through the quality of eternal life in the world now and the hope of resurrection from the dead in the world to come are intertwined throughout Paul's letters.

As Jesus's disciples had a glimpse of Christ's glory in his transfiguration before his resurrection, so we have assurances of eternal life now as we anticipate the culmination of our resurrection in the world to come. Again and again in his letters Paul reassures the faithful that ". . . if we have died with Christ, we believe that we will live with him" (Romans 6:8).

As I ponder the meaning of resurrection for my own life, the contradictions of time loom larger than those of physical space in my speculations about the contrast between my present body of flesh and my hope for a resurrected body of glory. Now in my eighth decade of life most of the cells in my body have been replaced numerous times. With the possible exception of certain neurons in my brain and some portions of my skeleton there is nothing left physically from my childhood in my present body. Thus in an analogous way it is not difficult for me to imagine the transmutation of the matter and energy of my present existence into something wholly new by God's grace and love, but in my existential musing the barriers of time seem much more formidable than the transmutations of physical matter into a resurrection body. Surely resurrection means more than an infinite series of sequential moments of time that begin after the last seconds of earthly breath and continue into eternity. Many people who have watched loved ones decline into states of babbling incoherence from diseases of senile dementia would not want that state to be perpetuated. People often speculate on regaining the physical strength of youth in their lives in the world to come, but I also would not want to be restored only to the callow insensitivity of my teenage years. Perhaps Christ gathers into what will be our risen bodies in the world to come all the moments from our earthly lives when we have come closest to knowing God, when God has transfigured us most nearly to the selves we were created and intended to be, and when Christ dwelt in us and we in Christ most fully.

Paul summarizes his hope for resurrection in the world to come emerging out of the quality of eternal life that we experience in the present world in his letter to his most beloved community of faith in Philippi. "But our commonwealth is in heaven, and from it we await a Savior, the Lord Jesus Christ, who will change our lowly body to be like his glorious body, by the power which enables him even to subject all things to himself" (Philippians 3:20–21 RSV).

When resurrection happens after death presents another conundrum for modern Christians. There is little question that both Jesus and Paul believed that human history would soon come to an end and that those who had died would remain in a coma-like state, something like the image of Sheol that Hebrew and Jewish people had believed for many years, until all were raised together.[6] In all three Synoptic Gospels, Jesus is recorded as saying that some people standing with him would "not taste death before the Son of man comes in power and glory" (Matthew 16:28; Mark 9:1; Luke 9:27). Yet, the world did not come to an end within a few decades or even a few centuries after Jesus's death and resurrection. The occasion for Paul's writing the first letter to the Thessalonians was their concern that people were dying, and there was perhaps already doubt even in Paul's mind that the world was soon coming to an end. Although Paul probably continued to believe in an imminent end to human history, he began to moderate his thinking in light of a possible extension of time. The Thessalonian letters are among Paul's earliest writings, but even here he affirms that whether we are awake (alive) or asleep (having died) we live through Christ (I Thessalonians 5:10).

The belief in the first century that human history would soon be over, shared by Jesus and Paul with many of their contemporaries, may be reckoned as one of Jesus's limitations in understanding that resulted from his full incarnation as a man who was subject to the boundaries of the knowledge of his time and of what was possible for a human being to know.[7] However difficult that may be for Christians to acknowledge and accept, the question remains whether the fullness of our resurrection will be deferred until the end of human history as the New Testament generally instructs or whether we share fully in God's kingdom in the world to come immediately after we die.

Although the dominant description of the resurrection of our bodies in the New Testament refers to an eschatological event (that is, an event beyond present history) at the end of the world, I never emphasized that message in any of the hundreds of funerals where I presided during five decades of ministry nor did I ever hear the doctrine of the "General Resurrection" enunciated at any funeral I attended in churches of any denomination. Perhaps it is best to leave our final outcome in God's hands with the hope and faith that what God has begun in us will be continued by a divine plan beyond our reckoning. Even Paul, who was intent on explaining everything, called it a mystery. "Listen, I will tell you a mystery! We will not all die, but we will all be changed, in a moment, in the twinkling of an eye, at the last trumpet. For the trumpet will sound, and the dead will be raised imperishable, and we will be changed. For this perishable body must put on imperishability, and this mortal body must put on immortality. When this perishable body puts on imperishability, and this mortal body puts on immortality, then the saying that is written will be fulfilled: 'Death has been swallowed up in victory.' 'Where, O death, is your victory? Where, O death, is your sting?'" (I Corinthians 15:51–55).

Although the sacrament of baptism was related to epiphany in the first chapter by the gift of our identity in our relationship to God, the origin of the process of indwelling whereby we are in Christ and Christ is in us is also symbolized and bestowed in the sacrament of baptism. In the Episcopal Church where most of those baptized are infants a few weeks or a few months old, I used the metaphor of a seed for baptism hundreds of times in instructing parents and godparents. The seed may grow and develop into a beautiful plant or it may wither and dry up and die. We can nurture and nourish the seed of baptism and the spiritual growth of the young tender plant of faith by prayer and spiritual instruction and above all through love and caring concern and interest, but like the growth of a beautiful plant in nature we cannot make it happen. Growth and development, like the formation of the original seed itself, come from a source beyond our ability to originate or control.

In the Episcopal Church we believe that the sacraments have an objective reality through the imputation of divine grace. Paul also implied that in baptism God bestowed the beginning of the process of incorporation into Christ and the initiation of eternal life, although the majority of those Paul baptized were probably not infants but were adults. "As many of you as were baptized in Christ have clothed yourselves in Christ Jesus" (Galatians 3:27).

In Paul's theology we are baptized into Christ's death, so that we can rise with him to eternal life (Romans 6:3). In the sacrament of baptism Paul associated the death of Jesus with the symbolic death of our old selves, damaged and diseased by sin. The motif of death is found not only in Paul's letter to the Romans but also in the language of baptismal liturgies in the church. "We thank you, Father, for the water of Baptism. In it we are buried with Christ in his death. By it we share in his resurrection."[8] One of the themes of the epistle of I Peter also relates baptism to martyrdom (and thus to death) as well as to the resurrection of Jesus. "By God's great mercy we are given a new birth into a living hope through the resurrection of Jesus Christ from the dead" (I Peter 1:3).

If the sacrament of baptism marks our official adoption by God as sisters and brothers of Christ through his incarnation and atonement and signifies the implantation of eternal life in us by Christ's indwelling in us and we in Christ, our rearing and growth in eternal life are marked and signified by the Eucharist. Unlike the single event of baptism—we are adopted by God only once—our nurture and nourishment in faith by God into fuller and more mature and complete eternal life are supplied often and regularly in holy communion. Once again to reflect out of my own tradition in the Episcopal Church, we believe that we participate objectively in the life of Christ by receiving his risen body and blood.

The Greek word for remembrance (*anamnesis*) used by Luke and Paul in their record of Jesus's institution of the Lord's Supper, carries a deeper meaning than the English translation. *Anamnesis* could more accurately be translated "unforgetting." As its derivative antonym, amnesia, in English means forgetting who we are, *anamnesis* means recalling both who we are and taking us back to the actual event with Jesus, much as the Hebrew people are taken back at Passover as if present themselves in the Exodus. (Eucharist and Passover are linked in many ways in the worship and historical memory of Christian people.) Even more than taking us back to be with Jesus, however, the Eucharist brings the Risen Christ into the world where we dwell now as Christ becomes present to us, with us, and in us in the bread and wine. Eucharistic prayers in the Episcopal Church petition God "that all who partake of this Holy Communion may worthily receive the Body and Blood of thy Son Jesus Christ."[9] Paul refers to the presence of Christ in the Eucharist with the rhetorical questions, "The cup of blessing that we bless, is it not a sharing in the blood of Christ? The bread that we break, is it not a sharing in the body of Christ?" (I Corinthians 10:16).

Much of the sixth chapter of John's Gospel elaborates the idea of the presence of the Risen Christ in the sacrament of holy communion. Although the words are quotations from Jesus, one must wonder if they are not more historically words of the Risen Christ, like many such passages in John's Gospel, as the author seeks to express the insights of faith arising out of Christ's presence with him in the sacraments. "So Jesus said to them, 'Very truly, I tell you, unless you eat of the Son of Man and drink his blood, you have no life in you. Those who eat my flesh and drink my blood have eternal life, and I will raise them up on the last day; for my flesh is true food and my blood is true drink. Those who eat my flesh and drink my blood abide in me, and I in them. Just as the living Father sent me, and I live because of the Father, so whoever eats me will live because of me'" (John 6:53–57).

Jesus's ordinance at the Last Supper that his disciples should drink the wine as his blood must have been shocking to them as well as scandalous to the first Jewish Christians. From ancient times the Hebrew people were forbidden to "eat" the blood even of animals, because the life or spirit of an animal was associated with its blood. The Hebrew word *nephesh* is translated as "soul" 428 times and as "life" 119 times in the King James Version of the Bible. In Leviticus 17:11–12 Moses relates God's commandment that because "the life of the flesh (*nephesh*) is in the blood . . . therefore, I have said to the people of Israel: No person among you shall eat blood, nor shall any alien who resides among you eat blood." Thus when the Synoptic Gospels and Paul quote Jesus as saying, "This cup that is poured out for you is the new covenant in my blood; do this as often as you drink it, in remembrance (*anamnesis*) of me," he was describing in the most radical and revolutionary way how they would receive and share his life and spirit (Luke 22:20, I Corinthians 11:25, cf. Matthew 26:27–28, Mark 14:24).[10] One of the accusations made about early Christians in the Roman world was that they were cannibals.

Because this book is my personal testimony of faith and hope, I have emphasized the sacraments, especially baptism and holy communion, which have become central to my perception of the presence of the Risen Christ within me and my sense of being incorporated into Christ. In the worship of the Christian Church, however, the sacraments are always conjoined with the word so that we receive Christ and are received into Christ within a context that also gives meaning and interpretation and understanding. Word and sacrament always go together. As a Baptist in my own earlier years well into my thirties, the word dominated. In fact, the word is dominant in many Protestant denominations. Just before the excursus on the Eucharist in the sixth chapter of John's Gospel, Jesus had said in the fifth chapter, "Very truly,

I tell you, anyone who hears my word and believes him who sent me has eternal life, and does not come under judgment, but has passed from death to life" (verse 24).

As Christ becomes present to us, with us, and in us in a particular and focused way in the Eucharist, we can believe that in a similar way the words that Christians speak when they are in Christ are in some sense also the words of the Risen Christ. An analogy might be drawn between our words becoming like the words of Christ and the bread and wine of Holy Communion that are being actually imbued with the real presence of Christ.

The transformation and incorporation of the lives of Christians into Christ reflect the meaning of "assimilation" by Albert Schweitzer when he remarks that the outward appearance of our natural existence is unchanged even as the outward appearance of the bread and wine remains unchanged. If we become Christ by sharing in the life of the Risen Christ, our words spoken in Christ are the words of Christ today, not only in sermons and churchly discourses but also in the shared conversations between Christian people. To be sure, our words are never the pure and wholly true words of God that Jesus spoke as God incarnate, because our words, even in Christ, are distorted by sin and marred by spiritual ignorance. We are becoming Christ and sharing in the life of God in Christ, but only Jesus was fully, completely, and perfectly God incarnate, and so only Jesus's words and actions revealed the pure and uncompromised love of God. Our words and actions in Christ also show God's love to a greater or lesser degree, however, as we are freed from sin and spiritual error and transfigured and incorporated more and more into Christ.

Recently I visited the Baptist church where I had served as associate pastor over four decades ago, when I had just graduated from seminary. As on most ordinary Sundays, there was no celebration that day of the Lord's Supper, but the presence of the Risen Christ was as palpable to me in the spoken and sung words as in my present Episcopal parish during the Eucharist. It is important to remember that Christ is present to us, with us, and in us through various means, and some people will respond to him and be found by him in one way more than in other ways.

It is both blasphemous and heretical to dictate how God may be revealed and enter into our lives. We cannot put limits on God's grace or presume to know the full activity of divine redemption in the world. God may come to people of non-biblical religions and be present with them in ways that Christians cannot understand or relate to. Although we can find common motifs with people of other religions in our experiences of epiphany and even in our transfigurations, as those terms are used here, when we affirm the presence of the Risen Christ in us and speak of how we are in Christ and so share in the life of God, it is more difficult if not impossible to express parallels with other religions. This is not to deny that people of other faiths may also share in God's life, but as Christians we can testify only to our own faith and can relate only intellectually (and even then poorly and partially) and not spiritually to the faith of other religions.

For us, as Christian believers, Christ is resurrection. In John's Gospel Jesus says to his friend Martha of Bethany, "I am the resurrection and the life. Those who believe in me, even though they die, will live; and everyone who lives and believes in me will never die" (John 11:25). In the first letter of John, the Christian affirmation that we can speak of our eternal life only in reference to Christ is elaborated. "This is the testimony: God gave us eternal life, and this life is in his Son. I write these things to you who believe in the name of the Son of God, so that you may know that you have eternal life" (I John 5:11, 13).[11]

Within the Christian community, however, the appropriation of the resurrection may take many forms and be expressed with varying emphases. Word and sacrament cover an enormous spiritual territory. The word is elaborated not only in endless verbal expressions but also in artistic representations from visual art to the aural forms of great music. In the controversies over the efficacy of icons as agents of the divine, the seventh ecumenical council (AD 787 in Nicaea) decreed that both word and image might lead to the knowledge of God.[12] Surely amid the modern controversies and squabbles of Christian denominations in the United States we might affirm that both sacraments and sermons may bring us into God's presence in Christ.[13]

During my visit to the Baptist church of my earlier life I was also reminded that sacramental actions through which the Risen Christ enters into our lives are broader and more diverse than their primary focus in the water of baptism and the bread and wine of holy communion or in the preached word. The sacrament of community is a spiritual action often experienced in the Church and in the world, and that sacrament of community was also palpable together with the Gospel of Christ's love and grace during my visit to Temple Baptist Church in Durham, North Carolina. The sacramental activity of Christian community will be an important aspect of what is meant by ascension in the following chapter.

The awareness of how we are being transfigured into the stature of Christ in our present lives gives us a sense of our resurrection and eternal life despite our limitations in the world now. As we hope for a perfect union with God in Christ when we shall share fully in the life of God in the world to come, we cherish the promises made to us by Jesus. For our lives in this world and for the world to come, however, eternal life means more than one individual person's relationship to Christ. The resurrection of the dead also involves the one holy catholic and apostolic Church on earth and the communion of saints in this world and in the world to come, all of which lead to a meditation on what I call ascension in the next chapter.

Notes

1 For a full explanation and history of the Hebrew and early Christian conceptions of resurrection, see Kevin J. Madigan and Jon D. Levenson, *Resurrection, The Power of God for Christians and Jews*, Yale University Press, 2008.

2 *The Mysticism of Paul the Apostle*, p. 130.

3 See Ian Curran, "Transformation," *The Christian Century*, July 15, 2008, Vol. 125, No. 14, p. 29, and William C. Placher, "How Jesus Saves," *The Christian Century*, June 2, 2009, Vol. 126, No. 11, p. 23–27.

4 *The Hymnal* 1982 (Episcopal), #488.

5   *The Mysticism of Paul the Apostle*, p. 110.

6   This belief was shared by Irenaeus (*Against Heresies*, chapter two, Bettenson, p. 110) and by Tertullian (*De Anima*, chapter fifty-five, Willis, p. 221–222) and probably by most of the other theologians in the first five centuries of Christian history.

7   This limitation of knowledge in Jesus is recognized by Athanasius. "Since He was made man, He is not ashamed, because of the flesh which is ignorant, to say, 'I know not,' that He may show that knowing as God, He is but ignorant according to the flesh." *Four Discourses against Arians*, chapter three, 43, Willis, p. 384.

8   *The Book of Common Prayer*, p. 306.

9   Ibid. Rite I, *Eucharistic Prayer II*, pp. 342–343; cf. Prayer I, p. 336.

10 Several insights in this paragraph are derived from a sermon by Stephen Elkins-Williams based on John 6:51–58 on August 16, 2009, the Eleventh Sunday after Pentecost, at the Chapel of the Cross in Chapel Hill, North Carolina.

11 The intervening verse (5:12) is deliberately omitted. While I agree that as Christians we can speak of eternal life only by referring to Christ, I cannot agree with the absolute exclusion of people from eternal life that do not acknowledge Jesus. The letter was written when some people within the Christian community were denying the incarnation of Christ and following a docetic doctrine, similar perhaps to those today that follow some of Jesus's teachings and "spirit" but deny his redemptive life, death, and resurrection as the Son of God. The letter says to them within the community of Christian faith that "whoever does not have the Son of God does not have eternal life," but I cannot apply those words today in our pluralistic society to people of other faiths outside the church.

12 See "Transformed," *The Christian Century*, p. 30.

13 Albert Schweitzer, who was a preeminent twentieth-century interpreter of J. S. Bach, drew a parallel between Paul's conception of eternal life in Christ and Bach's music. "The Christ-Mysticism Paul thought out within the framework of the eschatological world-view, with such depth and living power that, so far as its spiritual content is concerned, it remains valid for all aftertimes. As a fugue of Bach's belongs in form to the eighteenth century, but its essence is pure musical truth, so does the Christ-mysticism of all times find itself again in the Pauline as its primal form" (*The Mysticism of Paul the Apostle* 395).

Ascension

"You will receive power when the Holy Spirit has come upon you . . ."
— ACTS 1:8

"Very truly, I tell you the one who believes in me will do the works that
I do and, in fact, will do greater works than these, because I am going
to the Father." — JOHN 14:12

The accounts of the ascension of the Risen Christ in the Gospel of Luke and Luke's continuation of the story in the first verses of the Acts of the Apostles do not emphasize Christ's leaving so much as his followers' empowerment to carry on his work. During the years that Jesus trained his disciples, the central theme of his teaching was the kingdom of God. Paul uses the metaphor "body of Christ" to describe the Church and the phrase "new creation" to describe God's ultimate purpose for the world. The implications of the kingdom of God and the body of Christ and the new creation will be explored on the following pages. In pondering what ascension means as used typologically here for our Christian pilgrimage, the theme of power will be a recurring motif.

Although only Luke describes the event of the ascension of the Risen Christ, the reference to the ascension is often suggested in other New Testament books, especially in John's Gospel (e.g., John 20:17). The understanding of ascension emerges from the affirmation of indwelling which was explored in the previous chapter, "Resurrection": "On that day [when the Holy Spirit comes] you will know that I am in my Father, and you in me, and I in you" (John 14:20).

In truth this chapter could have been called (perhaps more accurately) "Pentecost" rather than "Ascension," because the Holy Spirit empowers the faithful to carry on Christ's work. In John's Gospel, Christ promises that the Spirit will abide with his disciples and be in them and teach them everything and remind them of all that Jesus had taught them (John 17:26). Because the overall theme of this book is "divinity in Christ," the title chosen for this chapter is "Ascension." The crucial role of the Holy Spirit, however, must not be forgotten in bringing the Risen Christ into the lives of the faithful and empowering the Church to continue the work of Jesus in the world as the body of Christ for the sake of the kingdom of God and the new creation. Because ascension points to the culmination of God's relationship with the world, it could also well be titled "Trinity," and indeed the roles of Christ and the Holy Spirit interdependent with the Father will be surveyed briefly at the end of this chapter.

Whether it is titled "Ascension" or "Pentecost" or "Trinity," however, one of the first questions concerns whether priority will be placed on what happens in the world now or rather at the end of human history. Ultimately the description of ascension in the typology of this book will involve both, just as both were involved in resurrection. The emphasis here, however, will be on what Christians are called to do in the world today and how they are empowered to fulfill their mandate.

The ascension event and its consequences, nevertheless, are associated with the end of human history, with what theologians call the eschaton. Just as the Risen Christ went away, he will come again. "This Jesus, who has been taken away from you into heaven, will come again in the same way you saw him go into heaven" (Acts 1:11, cf., Matthew 24:30 and I Thessalonians 1:10). There are numerous references to Christ seated at the right hand of the Father in heaven. The three Synoptic Gospels have different responses by Jesus to the question of Pilate at his trial, "Are you the Messiah, the Son of the Living God?" Some affirm Pilate's designation, and some evade a direct answer, but all three record Jesus's prophecy that people will "see the Son of man seated at the right hand of the Power of God" (Luke 22:67–69; Matthew 26:63–64; Mark 14:61–62).[1]

Power is the common theme that unites the prophesies of Christ's return at the end of human history and Christians' task of continuing the work of Christ within history now. In the various visions of Christ in heaven, references are made to his sitting at the right hand of power. Christians are empowered by the Holy Spirit to go forth proclaiming the coming Kingdom of God, living together in the body of Christ, and laboring for the new creation. The authority of Christ in heaven and on earth is linked to his commissioning disciples for the whole world: "All authority in heaven and on earth is given me. Go therefore . . ." (Matthew 28:19–20).

The continuation of Jesus's work in the world by his disciples is made explicit in Christ's prayer to the Father: "As you have sent me into the world, so I have sent them into the world" (John 17:18). The "Great Commission" in the last verses of Matthew's Gospel as well as the "High Priestly Prayer" in the seventeenth chapter of John are echoed in the appearance on the evening of the first Easter Day when the Risen Christ said to his disciples, "Peace be with you. As the Father has sent me, so I send you" (John 20:21).

The questions then arise: where are they being sent? For what purpose? What is their commission? What is the nature of their task and work? These questions lead back to the central metaphor of Jesus's teaching, the kingdom of God, and also to a reconsideration of his earthly ministry. One of the issues these questions raise involves whether God brings about the kingdom or whether Christ empowers his followers to bring the kingdom to the world. As was the case in considering whether the outcome of ascension refers to the end of history or to the present age, the answer is "both." Yet, the kingdom is primarily initiated and fulfilled by God. The liturgical ending of the Lord's Prayer states, "for thine is the kingdom and the power and the glory . . ." But Christians are called to participate and share in God's goal and purpose for the world in the realization of the kingdom.

One of the most difficult lessons throughout Christian history has been achieving a proper balance between what Christians are called to do and what they acknowledge as God's mysterious action in bringing about His kingdom on earth. It is crucial first to recognize that it is God's kingdom. "Thy kingdom come, thy will be done on earth as it is in heaven," is prayed even before the ascription to glory is affirmed ("for thine is the kingdom and the power and the glory"), in the Lord's Prayer.

Some eras of history have overemphasized the importance of human effort. Albert Schweitzer warned against the distortions of the late nineteenth and early twentieth centuries by Christians who sought to bring about the kingdom of God through social reform and solely human efforts.[2] The fulfillment of the kingdom of God can result only from divine initiative and divine action. Schweitzer refers to the perennial tension between our desires and efforts to bring about the kingdom of God and the mystery of God's time and purpose in its fulfillment. "In the hearts in which Paul's mysticism of union with Christ is alive there is an unquenchable yearning for the Kingdom of God, but also consolation for the fact that we do not see its fulfillment."[3]

The more frequent distortion during various centuries of the call to participate in God's work in the world in order to bring about the kingdom, however, has been a passivity that expects God to launch the divine kingdom on earth without any human effort or involvement. The best guide for an appropriate human role in sharing God's work in the world can be found in the teachings of Jesus about the kingdom of God as they are represented in the Synoptic Gospels. To be sure these teachings are clouded in mystery and enigma and paradox, as befits the struggle to understand and undertake responsibilities as God's human agents in His kingdom.

Volumes have been written about Jesus's references to the kingdom of God as recorded in the Synoptic Gospels. The brief comments that follow about Jesus's parables are my personal reflections in keeping with the theme of this book as a testimony of faith and hope, not a scholarly survey. Immediately after recounting Jesus's baptism and temptation, Mark introduces Jesus's ministry with his proclamation that "the time is fulfilled, and the kingdom of God has come near [or is at hand]" (Mark 1:15, cf., Matthew 4:17). Matthew's Gospel notes that when Jesus sent out his twelve disciples on their first mission unaccompanied by him, he gave them the same instruction with which he had begun his own public ministry: to proclaim as they go that the kingdom of heaven has come near (or is at hand) (Matthew 10:7).[4]

An adjunct message to the proclamation of the nearness of the kingdom is the injunction to wait with patience and anticipation for its advent, as illustrated in the parable of the wise and foolish bridesmaids (Matthew 2:1–13). When Joseph of Arimathaea took the body of Jesus to be placed in his own tomb, Luke described him as a man who "waited expectantly for the kingdom of God," which would seem to be the highest compliment that could be given to him (Luke 23:51).

What is said about this kingdom, other than its nearness, is cryptic and often puzzling. There are no observable signs to point definitively to the kingdom's emergence in the world and in people's lives, even though the kingdom is already "in the midst of us" (or "within us," as a possible translation) (Luke 17:20–21).

One dominant teaching enjoins us to seek the kingdom of God above all else (Matthew 6:33) and makes it the highest priority of our lives. Even parents and children are to be forsaken, if necessary, in order to enter the kingdom (Luke 18:29, cf., Matthew 19:29; Mark 10:29). In Mark's Gospel, Jesus probably uses hyperbole to say it is better for people to cut off a hand or pluck out an eye than to risk losing a place in the kingdom (Mark 9:47). Jesus's parables compare the kingdom to a pearl of great price and a treasure found in a field, which may also imply that in addition to its great value, it is discovered suddenly and even unexpectedly (Matthew 13:44–47).

Although people cannot do anything to produce the kingdom directly by their actions, Jesus's parables suggest that preparation for its reception is needed. It flourishes like plants in good soil (Matthew 13; 23; Mark 4:20; Luke 8:15). Even though people enter the kingdom with a certain awe and innocence like a child (Matthew 19:14; Mark 10:14; Luke 18:16), there is an ethical aspect to be observed in preparation for receiving the kingdom. God's commandments must not be compromised and righteous behavior must be maintained to be worthy of inheriting the kingdom (Matthew 5:17–20), which implies that the end does not justify the means in the quest for the kingdom, in spite of its being prized above all else. When a scribe affirmed Jesus's teaching that loving God and loving one's neighbor as oneself is more important than ritual worship, Jesus told him that he was "not far from the king-dom of God" (Mark 12:32). In the beatitudes Jesus taught that people must be spiritually eager ("poor in spirit" or "poor" in Luke's version) and meek to be able to receive the kingdom (Matthew 5:3; Luke 20). In another beatitude Jesus assured a place in God's kingdom for those who have been persecuted for righteousness's sake, whose rewards in heaven will be especially great (Matthew 5:10–12).

The ability to forgive others would seem to be an important condi-tion for entering the kingdom (Matthew 18:23–25), and compassion for the hungry and thirsty, naked, lonely, and imprisoned would seem to be essential (Matthew 25:31–46). Jesus promised that in his glory at the end of human history he would say to those who showed that kind of compassion, "Come, you that are blessed by my Father, inherit the kingdom prepared for you from the foundation of the world" (Mat-thew 25:34). Generosity would also seem to be a virtue of those who are eligible for acceptance into God's kingdom. People who have sold their possessions in order to give alms are welcomed into the kingdom (Luke 12:32), and those who cling to their possessions are unlikely to find the kingdom (Matthew 19:24; Mark 10:25; Luke 18:25).

Several of Jesus's parables suggest that working for the sake of the kingdom is required, but other than compassion and generosity it is difficult to determine what that work involves besides obedience to God. Empty pious talk will not be sufficient for entering the kingdom: not everyone who says "Lord, lord," is admitted (Matthew 7:2, cf., Luke 6:46). People are to work for the good of the kingdom diligently and faithfully as illustrated by the parable of the talents (Matthew 25:14–30; Luke 19:12–27), and yet some who labor little are rewarded more than those who labor long (Matthew 20:1–16).

Obedience and immediate response to God's summons would seem to be the most important requisites for people seeking the kingdom. In the parables of people invited to the royal wedding, those who made excuses and delayed were not admitted (Matthew 22:1–14, cf. Luke 14:16–24). Harlots and tax collectors who obey God immediately are more likely candidates for the kingdom than those who have kept the moral law scrupulously over the years (Matthew 21:31).

Jesus promised that the Holy Spirit would "guide you into all truth" (John 16:13), and that truth entails what God calls the faithful to obey in order to enter the kingdom. Ascension is thus a sharing in God's work as directed by the Holy Spirit.

There are several other aspects of the kingdom of God to be noted in Jesus's parables. Whatever our work following the Holy Spirit's leading may involve, human participation is a minor but necessary contribution to the outcome. The mustard seed produces a great bush, and a little leaven affects a great mass (Matthew 13:31–33; Mark 4:30–32; Luke 13:18–21). These parables imply that the human work for the kingdom is a tiny but essential element in the great and mighty work of God in the world.

Another of Jesus's dominant teachings involves a warning against a premature prediction of who is able to enter the kingdom and who is denied a place, as illustrated by the parables of the net cast into the sea bringing in every type and sort of fish and of the wheat and weeds, representing good and evil, not to be separated before the harvest (Matthew 13:36–43, 47–48). Jesus also taught that the kingdom would be universal; people would come from East and West, from North and South (Matthew 8:11; Luke 7:29). He also said that the kingdom would be unified and undivided (Matthew 12:25–27; Mark 3:23–26; Luke 11:17–18). In so far as the Church represents the nascent beginning of the kingdom in the present world (which will be discussed further below), it is described as "one" (undivided, embracing all of Christ's disciples) and "catholic" (universal) as well as "holy" (the work of God, not just a human effort) and "apostolic" (passed down faithfully from Jesus's first followers and disciples).[5]

Paul understood proclaiming the kingdom of God to be a major part of his role as the apostle to the Gentiles (Acts 19:8; 20:25), and the last verse of Acts pictures him "proclaiming the kingdom of God . . ."

(Acts 28:31). In his own letters Paul reiterates many of the aspects of the kingdom of God found in Jesus's teachings—that it involves not empty talk but powerful action (I Corinthians 4:30), that it is not about material comforts and possessions but "peace and joy in the Holy Spirit" (Romans 14:17 cf. I Corinthians 15:50), that suffering and persecution are related to sharing the work of the kingdom—a sentiment shared by John (Acts 14:22; II Thessalonians 1:5; Colossians 1:11–13; Revelation 1:9).

Not surprisingly Paul emphasizes the moral and ethical requirements for those who seek to inherit the kingdom of God by attaching to several passages long lists of those who cannot enter due to fornication, idolatry, adultery, prostitution, sodomy, theft, greed, drunkenness, reviling, robbery, impurity, licentiousness, sorcery, enmity, strife, anger, quarreling, dissension, envy, factionalism, carousing, and obscene and vulgar and silly talk (I Corinthians 6:9–10; Galatians 5:19–21; Ephesians 5:5). To his Gentile readers, who were not versed and immersed in the Hebrew moral law, Paul summed up his counsel, ". . . like a father with his children, urging and encouraging you and pleading that you lead a life worthy of God, who calls you into his own kingdom and glory" (I Thessalonians 2:11–12).

Paul, as well as James and John, echoed Jesus by contrasting the frequent poverty and weakness of those seeking God's kingdom with the riches and earthly power of the kingdoms of this world, which will be destroyed when God's kingdom is fulfilled and perfected on earth (I Corinthians 15:24; James 2:5; cf. Revelation 11:15; 12:10).

Paul suggested a new facet to the understanding of the kingdom of God in Colossians by referring to his companions as "co-workers for the kingdom of God" (4:11). The idea of the Church as the incipient kingdom of God is also found in the Revelation of John, where he writes that Jesus Christ has "made us to be a kingdom" (1:6) and that "you have made them to be a kingdom and priests serving our God . . ." in a hymn of praise to the lamb of God (5:10).

Referring to the Church as the body of Christ appears less like a metaphor than a literal description by Paul as he characterizes the embodiment of the Christian community in Christ. He never uses "the body of Christ" for an individual Christian person but rather always for the faithful community in Christ.[6] In the twelfth chapter of I Corinthians, Paul employs an extended allegory to illustrate that individual Christians cannot represent the body of Christ and that only in their unity can they be his body. "For just as the body is one and has many members, and all the members of the body, though many, are one body, so it is with Christ. Indeed, the body does not consist of one member but of many. If the foot would say, 'Because I am not a hand, I do not belong to the body,' that would not make it any less a part of the body. And if the ear would say, 'Because I am not an eye, I do not belong to the body,' that would not make it any less a part of the body. If the whole body were an eye, where would the hearing be? If the whole body were hearing, where would the sense of smell be?" (12, 14–17). As he develops his comparisons even further Paul suggests the incompleteness and inadequacy of individual Christians to be as Christ in the world but their completion and efficacy when they are incorporated together and "arranged" in Christ's body by God (18–26).

Once again as in the previous chapter, "Resurrection," so now in this chapter "Ascension," eternal life in, through, and with Christ is understood as a social and communal experience. Paul's most explicit statement is found in II Corinthians 12:27: "Now you are the body of Christ and individually members of it." The understanding of the body of Christ is expanded in Romans 12:5 to express the indwelling of the members of the Church with one another as well as together in Christ: ". . . so, we who are many, are one body in Christ, and individually we are members one of another." In Ephesians and Colossians the description of the body of Christ is modified by often calling Christ the head of the body, which is the Church (Ephesians 5:23; Colossians 1:18; 2:19).

Albert Schweitzer commented on this description of the Church by Paul: "The mystical Body of Christ is thus for Paul not a pictorial expression, nor a conception which has arisen out of symbolical and ethical reflections, but an actual entity. Only so can it be explained that not only can Christ suffer for the Elect, but also the Elect for Christ and for one another. This reciprocity of relations is founded on the fact that the existences in question are physically interdependent in the same corporeity, and the one can pass over into the other."[7]

Paul's sense of indwelling—Christ in him and he in Christ—was extended to those with whom he shared a ministry in the church. "God establishes us with you in Christ and has anointed us, by putting his seal on us and giving us his Spirit in our hearts as a first installment" (II Corinthians 1:21–22). The letters to the Philippians and the Colossians both begin with the greeting, "to all the saints and faithful [brothers and sisters] in Christ . . ." Paul can write of "speaking in Christ" as if Christ himself were speaking, and this sense of indwelling, which was discussed under the rubric of resurrection in the last chapter, is extended to what is meant here by ascension, as Paul incorporates others into this unity with Christ: "We (Paul and Titus) are speaking in Christ before God" (II Corinthians 12:19).

The affirmation of a communal resurrection, called ascension here, recalls an understanding of earlier Hebrew belief that endured in the first years of the Christian Church and rabbinical Judaism. "Many ancient Jews and Christians held, unshakably, that resurrection was a bodily and communal event. They understood the classic scriptural sources and heritages of both traditions to maintain that God would raise the dead in their full humanity, or as we should say today, as a physico-psycho-social unity."[8]

The new element in this belief, however, is the sense that eternal life is present now in earthly existence as a shared experience in community in relationship with others in Christ. In the New Testament this belief in shared life together in Christ as the Church receives its fullest expression in the book of Ephesians.[9] The letter affirms not only our being "made alive together in Christ" but also being "raised up with him and seated with him in the heavenly places." (2:5–6) Because the dominant metaphor for Christ's power and authority is expressed as sitting at the Father's right hand, the claim that Christians in the

Church sit with him in heavenly places implies that they also share his power and authority. The same metaphor is found in the fourth chapter, which then elaborates the gifts Christ gave to his followers. The one who "ascended far above all the heavens, so that he might fill all things" gave gifts that "some would be apostles, some prophets, some evangelists, some pastors and teachers, to equip the saints for the work of ministry, for building up the body of Christ, until all of us come to the unity of the faith and of the knowledge of the Son of God, to maturity, to the measure of the full stature of Christ" (Ephesians 4:10–13).

The goal of ascension for the faithful together in the Church according to Ephesians then is attaining "the full stature of Christ." The hope and purpose of the faithful are not only to be united in Christ in heaven but also to become fully and completely Christ in the world. While the ascension of the faithful is never perfected in the world so that they become fully and completely Christ in history, they continue toward that transformation in Christ and into Christ, not only as individuals but also as Christians together in the Church.

The creedal expression of this unity together in Christ as developed in Christian liturgy is often titled "the communion of saints." The union of disciples throughout the world in Christ now and their hope to be united with those who have already died and their participation all together even now in Christ are included in the full meaning of "communion of saints."

While the books of Ephesians and I Corinthians speak of apostles, prophets, evangelists, pastors and teachers as the roles that the ascended Christ assigns to those united to him in the Church of the first century, the sacraments that describe some of the roles of those united to Christ in the Church today are confirmation, marriage, and ordination. The designated roles in these three sacraments do not exhaust the ways and activities by which Christians are present in Christ to the world. They are representative, however, as Paul's lists are also probably not exhaustive but representative of how leaders were present in Christ within the early Church.

Not all Christians are called to a wedded union, but many, if not most, choose to live in a sanctified marriage. One of the prayers in *The Book of Common Prayer* for the Blessing of a Marriage is a petition for the couple to "make their life together a sign of Christ's love to this sinful and broken world . . ."[10]

Although baptism is the primary sacrament of Christian identity and initiation, confirmation represents the process of working out the specific actions of the baptismal covenant, which is always reaffirmed during the rite of confirmation and which in the Episcopal liturgy includes proclaiming "by word and example the Good News of God in Christ," seeking and serving "Christ in all persons, loving your neighbor as yourself," and striving "for justice and peace among all people" and respecting "the dignity of every human being."[11]

A distinguishing feature of this group of sacraments (confirmation, marriage, and ordination) is the intention in all of them of a lifelong commitment. That commitment in some people's lives may be renounced or withdrawn as a result of sinful circumstances. Other sacraments may then be involved, such as the reconciliation of a penitent, so that divine forgiveness is expressed and God's grace is assured. The lifelong intention in these sacraments, however, distinguishes them from other sacramental actions that are repeated and appropriate for an interim commitment of representing Christ in the world at important times in a Christian's life, for example, when finishing an educational milestone, graduating from high school, college, or advanced study, when undertaking a new vocation, when a child is born, before a major endeavor of mission or responsibility in the Church, and many more. It would be well to ask God's grace to lead, direct, and uphold the Christians who are on the "front lines" as lay people representing Christ to the world; these sacramental actions reaffirming baptismal vows and confirmation promises are designed for all who are ascended in Christ and live as those becoming Christ in the world and sharing Christ to the world.

Ordination is appointed for those who are called to permanent ministries in the Church. The diaconate somewhat connects the laity and the ordained ministries, because deacons ". . . make Christ and his redemptive love known, by [their] word and example" in "a special ministry of servanthood."[12] Thus deacons interpret "the needs, concerns, and hopes of the world" to the laity, who have a similar mandate to be in Christ and represent Christ in their daily lives among those with whom they live and work and play.

Priests and bishops always remain deacons within their specialized vocations in the church, as all three orders remain Christians who have been confirmed to continue exercising their baptismal covenants. Priests are ordained particularly to preach, to declare God's forgiveness and absolution and to administer the sacraments of holy communion and baptism.[13] In addition to all of these responsibilities, including their confirmation promises to uphold the baptismal covenant and their ordination vows for the diaconate and the priesthood, bishops are given the additional responsibility for ordaining priests and deacons and joining in the ordination of other bishops and having special roles in the leadership of the "Church throughout the world."[14]

In all of these roles within the Church and in the wider world the faithful are becoming Christ together, "ascending" even to be seated with Christ in the heavenly places, as Ephesians puts it. When a bishop lays hands on someone being confirmed in the Episcopal Church a prayer is made to "strengthen" and "empower your servant."[15] Once again the motif of power arises as it can be found throughout the process of our ascension in Christ.

After having considered the implications of the Christian Church as the body of Christ and as a prospective fulfillment of the kingdom of God, attention must be given to another of Paul's metaphors for sharing the work of God in the world, the metaphor of the "new creation," which was mentioned in the previous chapter. The phrase "new creation" is not as developed nor used as often in the New Testament as the "kingdom of God" and the "body of Christ," but the seminal idea suggested in Paul's letters supplies an especially important beginning point for the consideration of ecological theology, which is crucial for the situation of the present world. "In Christ there is a new creation: everything old has passed away; see, everything has become new!" (II

Corinthians 5:17). From the context of his declaration it may be assumed that Paul was thinking primarily about the human race as the new creation, but even in Paul's letters the metaphor implies a larger reference to the whole created order and harkens back to God's perfect creation before the Fall.

As early as the second century the prescient theologian who enunciated that Christ became human so that we might become divine saw the restoration of the whole created order in the idea of the new creation. Ireneaus wrote that ". . . this created order must be restored to its first condition and be made subject to the righteous without hindrance; and this the Apostle shows in the Epistle to the Romans, when he says, 'The earnest expectation of the creation awaits the revelation of the sons of God.'"[16] In this passage from Romans (8:18–25) quoted by Irenaeus, Paul writes about the whole creation "groaning in labor pains until now" awaiting the glory about to be revealed.

The image of the new creation is repeated in Galatians 6:15: ". . . the new creation is everything!" And in the first chapter of Colossians Paul develops most fully the idea of the new creation and its connection not only to the perfection of God's original creation but also to Christ in whom and through whom all things were created and will be restored. "For in him all the fullness of God was pleased to dwell, and through him God was pleased to reconcile to himself all things, whether on earth or in heaven, by making peace through the blood of his cross" (19–20).

The reconciliation of the whole creation in and to God leads to a consideration of the Trinity as Creator, Redeemer, and Sanctifier of the world. Augustine (of Hippo) described the Trinity as a communion of Father, Son, and Holy Spirit. "Call this friendship, if it helps, but a better word for it is charity (*caritas*) . . . and God is charity" (John 4:8, 16).[17] *Caritas* (love or charity) is one of the most "loaded" words in Augustine's writings. He uses this Latin word much as the Greek word *agape* is used today for the pure and perfect love of God as distinguished from human lusts, distortions, and desires. He even argues that ". . . the Godhead Itself is love," but *caritas* is especially associated with the

Holy Spirit as the bond between Father and Son (and yet substantive to each and all three, because God is One).[18]

Following Augustine, the contemporary theologian Harvey Cox has suggested that ". . . loving, including the neighbor, including the enemy, is an act of participation in the life of God."[19] In similar words Mary T. Clark's commentary on Augustine's Sermon on the Creed describes his image of the Trinity, as ". . . the love quality of inter-personal relationships. Fraternal love is a participation in the unity of God, in his intimate life; that intimate life is the life of Trinitarian relationships of love."[20]

The Trinity, as described by Augustine and his commentators down through the centuries, offers clues and language to describe our involvement in the life and work of God. The fellowship of Christians in the Church, at its best and most nearly perfect, participates in the life of the Trinity. The purest and truest righteous actions of Christians, especially in their life together in the Church, reflect the very love of God, which is the bond of *caritas* in the triune God. Participating in the work of God is the purpose of the Christian life in the world. Christians progress from knowing God to being transformed by God to sharing in the life of God to participating in God's work on earth.

Unlike other religions Christianity's goal is not just knowing God (enlightenment) nor being transformed by God (self-improvement or personal fulfillment) nor even sharing in the life of God (at least not in this world—the fullness of union with the Risen Christ in the world to come may be our ultimate destiny) but rather playing a role in God's plan for peace (*shalom*), justice, righteousness, and loving relationships on earth.

Although a spiritual progression may be traced in the Christian life from epiphany to transfiguration to resurrection to ascension, as those terms are used in this book, they are not always sequential in time. As Christians begin to labor in God's plan for the kingdom on earth, they may be given new epiphanies. As they are transfigured by imitating Jesus and receive the grace of the Holy Spirit, they may be united more and more fully into the Risen Lord. Participation in God's work in the world, however, relies on the foundation of the other spiritual stages. The Christian life is more than good works and social reforms, even those that fit the mandates of divine righteousness. Without seeing God in Christ and being transformed by God's love, good intentions and labor for just causes may soon burn out.

When we are in Christ and Christ is in us, we begin to participate in the work of God in the world. Although there may be instances when an individual Christian person becomes an agent in Christ of God's redeeming work, we are most often and most fully and most nearly in Christ as a Christian community, usually through the auspices of the Church. How ever much we fail and fall short of Jesus's example as individual Christians and as the Church, we seek forgiveness and renewal in our calling to be as Christ to the world today and to find our true divinity in Christ.

The Bible provides our job description, especially in what is highlighted by Jesus's ministry. As Jesus's first priority was the proclamation of God's kingdom, so our first priority in sharing God's work in the world is announcing God's plan and purpose of loving our neighbors as we love ourselves and also recounting the requirements of justice and righteousness involved in the kingdom. As Jesus taught us to love our enemies, we shall make God's peace (*shalom*) central to all that we say and do. As Jesus paid great attention to poverty and hunger, so shall we strive to alleviate poverty and hunger on the earth today as God's agents. As Jesus healed physical bodies and minds and souls, so shall we emphasize healing for all members of the human race. As Jesus calmed the raging sea and told stories about fruitful harvests, we are called to avert ecological catastrophe and provide sustainable nourishment for all the people of our world, not only now but for future generations as well. In everything we do, we shall treat all people with the dignity that befits those created in God's image, as Jesus did.

Nothing we do as God's agents in Christ today is the product of our good intentions and human efforts alone. As God encounters us and becomes known to us in Christ and reveals us to ourselves, the yearning is born in us to fulfill the divine plan and purpose for the world.

As we are transformed more and more nearly into the stature of the Christ, who was incarnated in Jesus, we are spiritually strengthened to fulfill our calling as those created in God's image. As we are united to Christ and to one another in Christ, we are given glimpses of eternal life in the world now and endowed with the hope of sharing fully and completely in the fellowship of the triune God through our eternal life in Christ in the world to come. And finally, as communities of faith in Christ, as the body of Christ on earth today, we are supplied with the grace and power to contribute our labors, however small and seemingly insignificant they may be, confident that God will use them and multiply them infinitely by divine power to bring the new creation and God's kingdom on earth as it is in heaven.

Christ is present in the world today allowing us to know God, transforming and conforming us into his image (for which we were created and intended to be), uniting us with himself and with one another, and empowering us as his body now on earth to contribute to the divine work and purpose of the new creation and God's kingdom. In our epiphany, transfiguration, resurrection, and ascension, however, Christ's presence among us, with us, in us often remains hidden and elusive, except in clues and signs for those with eyes to see and ears to hear and hearts to understand. I find some of those clues and signs in the following stories. It is my hope that anyone who reads ahead may also recognize them.

Notes

1 Matthew and Mark add, "and coming on [or with] the clouds of heaven." See also Acts 2:33–34, I Peter 3:22; and John 6:62, which echoes Psalm 110:1.

2 *The Mysticism of Paul the Apostle*, p. 388.

3 Ibid. p. 396.

4 Matthew consistently uses the phrase "kingdom of heaven" while all other accounts prefer "kingdom of God." Various explanations are offered for his unique terminology, among them that he thereby expresses the Hebrew reticence to use the name of God out of reverence.

5 "The Nicene Creed," *The Book of Common Prayer*, p. 328.

6   Paul always uses *soma* for the "body" of Christ in describing the Church, never using *sarx* in that description. See the discussion of *soma* and *sarx* in the chapter previous, "Resurrection."

7   *The Mysticism of Paul the Apostle*, p. 127.

8   Madigan and Levenson, *Resurrection*, p. 3.

9   Some biblical scholars question the authorship of Ephesians as coming directly from Paul, but it is certainly generally Pauline in being consistent with and developing upon his theology. For a discussion of this issue, see Paul Furnish, "The Letter of Paul to the Ephesians," *The Interpreters' One Volume Commentary on the Bible*, pp. 834–835.

10   *The Book of Common Prayer*, p. 429.

11   Ibid. p. 417.

12   Ibid. p. 543.

13   Ibid. p. 531.

14   Ibid. p. 517.

15   Ibid. p. 418.

16   *Adversus Haeresus*, chapter eight, 19–20, Bettenson, p. 136.

17   *The Trinity*, Book VI: 7, translated by Edmund Hill, New City Press, 1991, p. 209.

18   *Faith and the Creed*, chapter nine, translated by Robert P. Russell, The Catholic University of America Press, 1955, p. 338.

19   "Shifting Discourse," *Harvard Divinity Bulletin*, Autumn 2008, Vol. 36, No. 3, p. 13.

20   Augustine of Hippo, *Selected Writings*, Paulist Press, 1984, p. 44.

Country Boys

O ld Man River" was utterly unsuited for David when he auditioned for a solo in the chorus. He had a light, rather pleasant but unremarkable baritone voice. Yet, I couldn't fiddle with my note cards, as I usually did to disguise the lack of interest reflected on my face—I was never good at hiding my reactions.

His eyes held my attention, not so much their clear blue color as their intensity and setting in deep sockets like holes in his angular face with its high cheekbones and sunken cheeks. The eyes inside his face were like the fervent voice within his thin, almost frail body, both unsupported and seemingly isolated from his other parts. After all he was only a sophomore. Perhaps he would develop diaphragm muscles and put on some weight in a couple of years and thereby gain vocal resonance.

As I usually did, I asked David to repeat the melody I played for him on the piano and then to improvise on its theme. This three-minute exercise was devised to spare the feelings of those auditioning for solos from an immediate blunt rejection, but never before had a student, trained or untrained in music, demonstrated such subtlety and invention, and dare I say it, such genius.

It was then that I heard the concealed mystery of his voice, like an echo heard in a cave at a great distance.

"David, I'm not sure you're quite ready for a solo this fall, but I like to work with all those I'm considering for a few weeks before I make a final decision. Would you be able to come for a voice lesson after school a couple of times for the next week or two?"

"Oh, yes sir, Mr. Harris. I'll git over here ever when you say to." If he had been a puppy he would have been licking my face.

"Tuesdays and Fridays at three forty-five suit you?"

"Oh, yes sir. Lack I said, ever when you tell me." (Note to myself: first attention must be given to correcting that country twang in his pronunciation.)

DURING THE FOLLOWING TWO WEEKS on Tuesday and Friday afternoons I could hardly wait until I arrived at home in order to tell Elaine about David's lesson. "He's unbelievable. I've never had a prodigy before. He's never studied theory a day in his life, but he understands inversions and diminished intervals—everything—just by intuition. I'm beginning to bring his voice out, too, and it's lovely. Charming. Sweet, if you can say that about a baritone. Not like Scott's, of course. There's never been a voice like Scott's in my experience. If I could just put them together, Scott's voice and David's musical brilliance . . . ! Both in the same year, and I'll have them both together again next year, if they sign up for the chorus. Can you imagine. . . !"

Scott's lesson came just before David's, right after the last school period in the afternoon, so that he would have time to arrive at football or basketball or baseball practice—whatever the season might be— only a few minutes late. Sometimes I marveled at how Scott kept all the plates of his activities spinning in the air simultaneously. Not only was he president of his class and usually captain of whatever school team was in season, but he also had the athletic physique and rugged good looks that attracted the girls' attention. He seemed to "go steady" with a different sweetheart every month, as if he was obligated to date every pretty girl in the school and get to several bases with each one of them, as the students put it in the gossip about the physical stages of their courtship rituals.

With his flurry of interests I was grateful that he'd continued to sing in the chorus into his third year of high school. At times I caught myself in a fawning, obsequious demeanor in dealing with Scott, as almost everyone else responded to him, teachers and students alike, but he enjoyed singing the solos and being center stage and the object of everyone's attention. He knew that his pure, clear tenor voice was remarkable and beautiful. He was never nervous, never suffered from stage fright in a performance; there wasn't a shy bone in his body.

It was ironic that tall, muscular Scott possessed a lyric tenor voice while thin, frail David was a baritone. It took endless lessons to teach Scott the melodies for his solos. The only common trait between the boys was their twang: both of them country boys. Scott often encouraged David as they met between their lessons and always took time to speak kindly to him, unlike many of the students who teased David unmercifully for his gawkiness; there wasn't a mean bone in Scott either.

BOTH BOYS had been born during the war, when we were fighting the Germans and the Japanese, into families from out in the county that had suffered during the Great Depression. Both families watched their expenditures very carefully, but Scott's father was a fairly prosperous farmer who could afford to pay for Scott's voice lessons. After the third week I wrestled with the dilemma of continuing or stopping David's lessons. I suspected that my fees would be a burden for his family.

"David, I can't give you a solo yet, but I'd like to keep working with you and hope that you'll be able to solo in the spring or next year. I'm going to offer you a scholarship to continue your lessons twice a week, if you'd like to."

"Golly! Gee whiz, Mr. Harris, you know I would if'n yo're willing, but Pa'ud pay you, I reckin."

"This year you'll be a scholarship student." But the thought of his father's willingness to pay gave me another idea.

THE FOLLOWING WEEK I was able to follow through on the notion. The algebra teacher pointed out David's parents to me at a PTA meeting, and they looked just as I'd imagined them. His father stooped forward with slumped shoulders and the gaunt face and the thin, bent frame that David had inherited. His mother bent in the opposite direction with a swayback that caused her neck to bulge out in front. She crossed her arms over her ample breasts and tossed her head back and forth as if the plaited bun on her crown was a bird's nest on a limber branch whipped by the wind.

"Hello, I'm Mr. Harris, David's choral director and voice teacher."

David's mother smiled broadly, and his father smiled faintly, but probably as broadly as he ever smiled, and, as I expected, his mother did all the talking. "We're proud to meet up with you. That's all David can ever talk about, you and that there choir of you'rn."

"He's a remarkable boy. He has real gift. I think he could be a fine musician. I don't think I've ever had a student with a talent like his."

She beamed, and her husband almost beamed, too. I suspected that like his smile, it was as exuberant an expression, however pale, as he was capable of showing. "We're right stuck on David. He's our only chile, you know. He's always loved music and singing in church."

"He really needs to study piano. Even for vocal music, everyone should know some keyboard and theory." I realized that I'd lost them with the references to "keyboard" and "theory," so I kept on talking. "Do you think you'd be willing to pay for some piano lessons for him?"

"How much'ud that come to?" David's father spoke at last.

"I charge two dollars a lesson. I'd like to have him twice a week, right after his voice lessons."

"That's a whole lot. Four dollars a week." David's mother pursed and unpursed her lips as she spoke. I was about to offer another scholarship, but I was wary of insulting their country pride.

"We can manage that . . . fer David, Ma."

"I reckin so. Yeah, awright."

PERHAPS I WAS OVERLY FAMILIAR with my private students to whom I gave lessons in voice and piano during the afternoons after their classes ended; or perhaps it was due to their unwinding after the tensions and stresses of the day, but most of them revealed their confidential secrets in between the musical pieces they rehearsed. Surprisingly, Scott, who always appeared to be the picture of self-confidence and leadership in public, began to expose his doubts and insecurities in my studio.

"I don't like jumping from one sport to another ever' month, ya know. I'd just like to focus on one thang long enough to appreciate what I'm a'doing. My folks they want me to do ever'thang, and I'd like to do just one thang well enough to do it real good."

"I hope you aren't thinking about giving up chorus and voice lessons, Scott." And I hoped my panic didn't show.

"Oh, no sir. I ain't about to give up my music. It's the one thang that always makes me feel happy. I just worry that if'n I give up something else, people won't like me for it."

"It's important for people to like you, isn't it, Scott?"

"Yeah, I reckin so." Then he picked up his sheet of music to sing and signaled that the personal revelations had come to an end for today.

Unsurprisingly, David expressed the same kinds of anxieties and insecurities in my studio that he manifested in public, but when he turned to the pieces of music he was practicing, he became calmly in control, even masterful. Within the first three months of studying the piano, he had progressed to a level usually attained by my students only in their third or fourth year of study.

"Where do you practice, David? I don't think you have a piano at home, do you? I've heard you on the piano in the auditorium waiting for your bus in the afternoons, but that gives you less than an hour or so. Is that the only practice you get between our lessons?"

"Oh, no sir. I walk down to the church and practice most ever' night after I he'p Pa finish the chores. Sometimes he'll come down there to fetch me, 'cause I fergit how late it's getting. I guess I'd druther be with a piano than with people. I reckin people don't like me very much."

"Surely that's not true, David. Scott seems to be very fond of you. He always says nice things about you, even before you come in at the end of his lesson."

"That's so. Scott's always real nice to me. I think he's prob'ly the nicest person I ever knew. He acts different from ever'body else towards me."

Like Scott, David turned away from me toward his music and actually began playing the piano to conclude our verbal conversation, but the emotions he had awkwardly expressed in his spoken words continued with refined eloquence in his music, even in the simple études of a beginner's book. He seemed to bring inner depths of meaning and passion even out of the simplest of tunes.

FOR THE SPRING CONCERT César Franck's *Panis Angelicus* seemed to me an ideal duet for Scott and David. I asked David to come for the last ten minutes of Scott's lesson and asked Scott to stay a few minutes longer each week, so that they could practice together. Perhaps Scott's robust tones and deep natural breaths would help David, whose voice was still weak and shallow inside his body. Perhaps David's phrasing and sensitivity to dynamic levels would inspire Scott, who tended to sing everything *forte* or *mezzo forte*.

Their voices did blend together beautifully, although Scott tended to drown out David. "Scott, I want you to take it down a notch or two. Sing as softly as you can. Here, David, put your hand on Scott's diaphragm as he sings and feel how he breathes." David obeyed me, and as Scott began to sing, David turned beet red in the face, and Scott began to laugh. "Okay, okay, that's enough. You get the point."

THE NEXT WEEK Scott seemed rather glum when he arrived for his lesson, although he never appeared to wander far toward either elation or depression from the medium of pleasant normality. "Well, yo're cursed when you git what you ax fer, I guess. Daddy he wants me to pick jus' one sport this spring fer my senior year so'as I can try to git me a scholarship to play at the university."

"That is kind of what you said you wanted, isn't it? What's the matter? You aren't dropping chorus, are you?" I was afraid I might sound desperate again.

"No way. If'n I play sports in college, I won't have no time to do nothing else. I'm not sure I can keep my grades up enough to even stay in school. It's fer sure they won't let me sing in the glee club or choir. They say you have to practice all the time if'n yo're on a college team."

"Scott, you're a straight A student, aren't you?"

"Near about, I reckin."

"I don't think you'll have to worry about flunking out of college."

"They say college is a whole lot harder than high school, Mr. Harris. I don't know if I wanna practice ball four or five hours a day. It's all I can do to keep up now."

"You'll be all right." I thought, 'You're the kind of boy that always comes out on top.'

David was frustrated by the joint rehearsal time with Scott. Although he beamed fawningly at Scott during their time together, he refrained from mentioning anything personal in Scott's presence, and he had to catch his bus immediately after his lesson, so that the time to talk with me after going over his pieces was limited.

One afternoon, just as David was about to leave, he blurted out, "I don't have no friends. Nobody in this here school likes me."

"Don't you think Scott likes you?"

"I dunno. I reckin. I like Scott a lot."

"Why don't you let him know that?"

"I dunno. Maybe. I gotta go catch the bus."

Someday this school will hire a guidance director and a vocational advisor, but without anyone in those positions now, students often come to me, not just those studying music privately with me and not even just those in the school chorus. I fancy myself to be something of the unofficial counselor for the school, and I suppose my students must recommend me to their peers, some of whom I don't know at all but who appear at my studio door seeking advice. If my own students don't mention their course selection and future educational goals, I raise those issues with them toward the end of each academic year, especially with juniors like Scott.

"Have you picked the sport you're going to focus on? Or is it still your plan to work on one more than the others?"

"Yes sir, my Daddy keeps after me to do that, and I'm gonna drop out of spring practice fer football. I'm gonna keep on running track, because I like it better 'an anything else, but Daddy he says you can't get no scholarship fer track, and I like baseball next best, so I reckin it'll be baseball. I ain't gonna go out fer basketball and track next year though."

"That sounds like a plan. Have you thought about what you'd like to study in college?"

"Daddy he wants me to major in business administration. He says it's the best chance for gettin' a good job wherever you settle down to live."

"Well, when you get to college you may discover something that interests you a lot, something you get really passionate about. That often happens. College students often change their majors once they're exposed to higher education. You should keep an open mind." As much as I wanted to tell Scott to be his own man and not become locked into the narrow rut that his father had predestined for him, I knew better than to contradict parental guidance at this stage of his life.

IT WOULD HAVE BEEN NATURAL for David's vocational goals to be vaguer and more romantic than those of an upperclassman. A year makes a great deal of difference in the maturity of high school students. Freshmen and sophomores often talk about being foreign missionaries or opera singers or even movie actors. I expected to hear such delusional nonsense from David, but he was both definite and down to earth as he spoke about his life's work.

"I'm a'hoping to be the minister of music and lead choirs in churches, if'n I can git to college a'tall, and you know that's a mighty big 'if.'"

"I think you have a very good chance of going to college, David." I wanted to tell him, 'I'm going to do everything in my power to make that happen,' but discreetly refrained from saying that I'd already planned to set up an audition for him with Professor Hodgson at the university. "Have you ever considered other kinds of music—university teaching or composing or directing an orchestra or even concert performance?" With David, unlike with most freshmen and sophomores, it was more a matter of expanding his horizons and suggesting his unlimited potential than dampening romantic fantasies.

"I don't mean no disrespect to you, sir. I think teaching is a wonderful profession, but I think we ourghta use all our talents in the church in these here times. I'm not sure anything on the earth will last much longer."

"What do you mean by that, David?"

"Well, what with the Russians having the atomic bomb and gettin' into outer space ahead of us . . . I just don't think our country will last much longer. Do you think they're gonna take us over?"

"No. No, David, I don't think so. Not at all."

"Well, I hope yo're right. I jus' believe I'm not gonna live to be an old man or even as old as my Ma an Pa."

David had often spoken of his fear of the Russians and seemed to be preoccupied with his death. I credited such somber forebodings to a combination of his feelings of personal insecurity and the apocalyptic sermons he heard in his country church. I was aware that my dreams for David's future in the musical world were as fanciful as the visions his classmates imagined for their futures. One of my daydreams pictured David conducting the orchestra at the Metropolitan Opera, perhaps premiering one of his own compositions and turning to recognize me in the audience as his teacher.

THE SPRING CONCERT that Friday night was the highpoint of my career. Scott had learned to modulate his voice and anchored the tenor section, and David's voice had finally emerged, not as strong as Scott's, but so pure and true that it guided the rest of the basses. The Franck duet was truly the jewel in the crown of the evening. After Scott and David sang, there was a hushed moment of absolute silence before the thunderous applause.

After the concert Scott put his arm around David's shoulder and slapped him in the belly—on the spot where David's hand had touched Scott's diaphragm when David had blushed deep crimson—the same way Scott congratulated a teammate who had scored a touchdown on the football field or hit a homerun on the baseball diamond. "Great going, buddy! That was awesome!" Never before had I witnessed a look of such sheer bliss and joy on David's face, that echoed my own feelings as people offered their gracious, superlative compliments to me about the concert.

THE MONDAY AFTER THE CONCERT David was missing from my fourth period choral class and when I stopped by the principal's office after school, I learned that he had been absent for the whole day.

When David didn't come to school again on Tuesday and Scott came for his private voice lesson after the last class period, I asked if he knew whether David was sick.

"I got a suspicion he couldn't face up to me."

"Why? You both seemed so happy and proud of yourselves after the concert."

"Yes sir. Some of us was goin' out to celebrate, and I axed David to go along with us."

"Did he go?"

"Yes sir. That's when the trouble started."

"What kind of trouble? What happened?"

"I'd druther not talk about hit."

"I won't repeat anything you tell me, but I'd like to be able to understand . . ."

"Jest fergit hit."

"Scott, I'd hoped you could trust me enough . . ." As we looked at each other during the uncomfortable silence, Scott squirmed as if he needed to get something off his chest.

"Well, awright then. Whenever we got to the Greenlight Inn, he come up to me in the men's room and told me he liked me and offered to go down on me. I told him I didn't like queers and for him to leave me alone."

"Have you told anyone else about this? I think it would make it hard for David . . ."

"No sir, I don't talk about them things. I ain't told nobody but you, not even my daddy."

What could I say? My heart was pounding, and I was almost in tears. I felt queasy. My stupid, fanciful dreams of mentoring a masterful musician fell apart like a stack of pick-up-sticks, but my deeper sadness focused on David, who might be prevented from fulfilling his great potential if he was branded publicly as a homosexual. "David's very immature, you know. Boys go through these phases sometimes growing up."

"That ain't no excuse. There ain't no excuse fer that kind of thang. I told him all his big talk about leadin' choirs in church was crazy. Warn't no church gonna have a little two-faced faggot like him leadin' its choir. I told him 'at I didn't never want to see his face ag'in."

"That's awfully harsh, Scott."

"I don't kere. He had it a' comin' to him. He better not never come around me ag'in. I don't never want him to look me in the face ag'in."

"I think we'd better skip your lesson today, Scott. I don't believe I feel much like teaching after what you've told me."

"That suits me just fine. I don't feel much like singin' today neither."

BY THE TIME that school opened on Wednesday morning everyone had heard the news. I despised the girls who had never given David a second glance and now huddled in each other's arms in the hallways and wept and wailed as if they'd lost their dearest friend. At least the boys walked around with vacant stares in stony silence reflecting their feelings of confusion and bewilderment.

David's father had assumed that he had walked down to their church to practice the piano after his evening chores, as he usually did. He had told his parents that he didn't feel well enough to go to school on Monday and again on Tuesday morning, but by the late Tuesday afternoon, he had told his father that he felt well enough to help him in the barn. When it grew late, his father had gone to the darkened, empty church and then on some ominous premonition had returned by way of the barn and found David hanging from one of the rafters with his worn belt around his neck. His blue jeans had slipped off his narrow waist and fallen around his buttocks exposing his underbriefs.

The old, frayed belt had almost broken in two from his weight and had snapped halfway to one of the notches. If only it had broken completely and spared his life!

That Wednesday Scott was also absent from school, and even though he returned to school on Thursday, he didn't attend the glee club practice. On Friday he opened the door of my studio without knocking—something he had never done before at the time for his lesson. "Can we jus' talk? I still don't feel like singin'."

"Of course, Scott."

Scott began to weep. He didn't speak for a long time. He brushed away his tears with the backs of his hands, as I would have expected him to do in the common athletic gesture for wiping off sweat. Then he began to sob and wail. He sounded like a girl or a very little boy. In any other circumstance I would have comforted him and put my hand on his shoulder, but I couldn't touch him; my anger was too great. Finally, he hushed and looked straight into my face with his red swollen eyes. "It was my fault. I kilt him sure as if I hung him up there myself."

I wanted to say, 'You're damned right you did. That's exactly what you did. I blame you. I hate you for it.' But I restrained myself and mouthed the appropriate, expected words. "You can't blame yourself, Scott. You're not responsible for what David did to himself."

"You know good and well I am. Yo're the only one what knows. I ain't told no one else, not even my Daddy, and now I never can."

"Perhaps we all contributed to what happened. I might have done something if I'd understood David better." Scott was leading me into a deeper truth about my own arrogant complicity.

"Not like me. I'm the main one."

THE FUNERAL was more dreadful than I could even have imagined. When the preacher tried to make David's death into a moral lesson for teenagers about the fate of not believing fully and completely in Jesus, I closed my eyes and bit my lip to keep from screaming at him. Most of the students couldn't fit inside the little country church, but through a window opened to allow a breeze to come into the hot, sticky air inside the church I could see the girls on the lawn huddled into their knots of three and four, holding each other's shoulders and wailing like a fake Greek chorus. The boys maintained their vacant, dazed, bedeviled stares, except for Scott whose face was twisted into a shape like a tormented gargoyle.

It was hard to distinguish what was sweat and what were tears streaming down the red plump faces of the country women who fanned themselves slowly with the squares of cardboard attached to popsicle sticks with black lettered funeral home advertisements on one side and colored biblical scenes on the other side. David's mother wore a black dress that appeared to be very old, and his father had donned black trousers and shiny black shoes and a white shirt that seemed to have been bought just for this day. Their bodies were the color of the wooden unpainted walls of the church, and it was remarkable that their tears or any moisture could flow from anything so dead and dry. Their faces, unlike Scott's face, were not twisted and tormented by grief; they seemed utterly worn out and empty, like the ragged denim clothes they had worked in until they were ready to be thrown away. They had lost everything. There was no use for them any longer.

After the interment David's mother approached me and told me how much David had loved his study of music with me and related the awful details that she had learned from her husband about how David's body had appeared in the barn. Her husband was now even more silent than ever, as if he might never speak again. I embraced her gently and shook hands with David's father and muttered, "I loved him, too," then slipped away. I saw her nod to Scott as if beckoning him toward her, but he turned and fled before he could be summoned.

THE FOLLOWING WEEK Scott didn't come to his choral period nor to his private lessons. He evaded me in the hallways between classes, but I didn't report his absences to the principal's office. The last days of classes fell during the next week, just before final exams and the summer vacation would begin. On Monday, Scott came to the fourth period choral class but avoided looking at me, and after school he knocked on the door of my studio almost before the bell stopped reverberating. His face no longer appeared twisted and tormented. I observed a calm serenity and assurance in his countenance that I'd never seen in him before.

"I wanted to tell you what all I decided."

"What's that, Scott?"

"I told my Daddy I'd play baseball at college if that'ud he'p him pay fer my tuition, but I was gonna major in music."

"Really! I knew you liked to sing, but I had no idea you loved music that much."

"I do love it, but I gotta do it fer David, so as I can be a minister of music in a church like he wanted to." We were silent. I didn't know how to reply. We looked into each other's eyes. I realized after a while that we were both smiling. "Course I know I won't never be good as David could've been."

"You've only got to be as good as Scott can be. You've got your own talents and gifts."

"Yeah, I reckin people sorta look up to me and foller me. I guess I might encourage 'em some, like you did fer David and me." The once oblivious boy who had lived only in the glow of his popularity and attractiveness now seemed to be growing aware of both his true strengths and limitations.

"You're a natural leader, Scott. You have the gifts to inspire people and foster their enthusiasm whether in the church or somewhere else."

"I reckin it'll be at church, like I said. Oh, I fergot to tell you, last Sunday I went and joined the church. Brother Sewell he's gonna baptize me next month, along with the others. Most of 'em are younger than me, twelve or thirteen, one's just barely ten, that joined the church during the revival. I never had a notion to join the church 'til now. 'Til after David's . . ." He paused, but I couldn't think of anything to say in response at that moment. "I guess the spirit just come on me sudden like last Sunday. I promised to foller Jesus when I went down during the invitation hymn, and part of that seemed like promising to be a minister of music like David wanted to."

"How did you become so wise so young?"

"You know better 'an I do how." His face became stern, even severe and bellicose. "I still got to catch up learnin' about music. Would you be willing to give me piano lessons this summer and next year like you did fer David?"

"Of course."

He began to weep and so did I. "He was yore prodigy, that's what you called him, and I took him away from you. Maybe someday I'll have me one, when I get to be a teacher like you, and won't go an' lose him."

Then he began to quake and wail like the girls in their Greek chorus, but Scott's cries bore nothing false, nothing fake. I stood and walked over to the piano bench where he was sitting and folded him into my arms, with his big hands and huge muscular biceps two or three times larger than mine pressed against my chest, but he felt like a baby, sobbing almost like a newborn on my shoulder.

A Higher Power

Martha's testimony

Driving through this part of town by herself didn't bother Martha during the daytime. At night she would have been uncomfortable alone in the car. As she came around a corner too fast the grocery bags tilted and almost turned over on the seat, and she had to reach out with her right arm to hold them and keep them from falling off onto the floorboard, the way her mother had reached over to hold Jake and her when she'd slammed on the brakes, the way Martha would have caught the babies she had never had. The advantage of coming in the daytime was not feeling afraid and uneasy. The disadvantage was seeing all the trash on the streets and sidewalks. At night she wouldn't see the littered papers and empty bottles, but Frank's anger would be beside her in the car, when he insisted on accompanying her after dark. Even when he refused to speak, as he usually did on these errands, she could feel his resentment, especially in his sullen silence, a silence three times as heavy as anything he'd ever said to her.

As she turned into Jake's street, she saw him in front of a neighbor's house, helping to load a refrigerator or a washing machine or some kind of big white boxy appliance onto a broken down pickup truck. He strained to nudge the washing machine onto the bed of the pickup—she could see that it was a washing machine now. The glistening sweat on his arms and shoulders clothed him in a bright light. He almost never took off his shirt, not because he was ashamed of his body, more out of modesty, not wanting to show off and let people think he was proud of his chiseled muscles.

Jake was always ready to lend a hand to anyone needing assistance.

Almost the first words she could remember his speaking were "Can I help?" when he was only two or three years old, her little brother, four years younger. Everyone said he was a good-hearted man. People who became drunks often seemed to have a generous, kind nature; maybe that was part of the same genetic make-up that disposed them to drink by feeling the sorrows and pains of the world more than other people did. After all, she'd experienced some of the same losses and hurts that Jake had, although all the things that had happened to him had been horrible, far worse than her suffering, but they were no excuse for how he lived now. He would do anything for you, even for a stranger, give you the shirt off his back, if you were in trouble. If he would accept just half of the help he offered to other people, maybe he could lick his addiction. Many's the time she'd offered to help him—Frank, too—and all sorts of other people. She even asked him if she could bring her preacher by to talk with him. (If only he would trust Jesus to help him!) Still, in the four years she'd been trying to take care of him—the same length of time as the difference in their ages—she'd seen him drunk no more than three, maybe four times. He was a binge drinker. He didn't stay drunk all the time.

"I'll just take these groceries on in the house."

"Thanks, Sis, I'll be there in a minute." He grinned.

Nobody could grin like Jake. It was not a big, toothy grin, but the whole world lit up, and you felt warmer and brighter just for being around him. He could have been really something if he hadn't been ruined by alcohol, probably lots of other drugs, too. Martha resisted the impulse to search the house, while he was still outside, for bottles or worse things, illegal things. What good would it do? What could she do if she found them except make herself miserable?

"Sorry I'm such a mess." He was wearing an undervest. After he grew up she'd never seen him without some sort of shirt on unless he was swimming, and even then, he stayed down in the water most of the time. He mopped his face and neck with the wadded up faded blue denim shirt that he'd pull off. He could never abide being dirty, even as a little boy. He was forever running inside to wash his hands and face. How could he apologize to her for a little dirt and never say a solitary word of repentance about his addiction? "You don't need to bring me all this stuff. I got food, and I'm working now and drawing a regular paycheck." Jake never had trouble getting a job and usually worked his way up to a good position in a short time, until his next big drunken binge, when he would be fired.

"You don't have any home cooking though. There's nobody to cook for you, looks like there never will be the way you're going, and I know you're not about to cook for yourself."

"And you know how much I enjoy it and appreciate it." He grinned, and the room lit up. It was always like this between them. Martha would fuss and nag, and Jake would take no offense, and her heart would melt. He could win anybody over, like a little lamb, her little brother. Why hadn't this loving little lamb won some good woman's heart who would love him and take care of him and reform him? Lord knows, enough had tried. (She remembered Helen but immediately pushed the thought out of her mind.)

"The casseroles are all cooked. All you have to do is put 'em in the toaster oven for a few minutes and warm 'em up. And I baked some butterscotch squares in the tin there."

"Mama's butterscotch brownies. My favorites." The grin faded, and he scowled. Both of them felt the pleasant pain and the mournful joy of remembering. Other people could eat the butterscotch brownies that Martha often baked and gave away, but only the brother and sister could really share them. Certain things only a brother and sister could share. Frank would never be able to understand that bond.

"What are you working at now?"

"I got a job at the filling station over on Cypress."

"You like it?"

"It pays the rent."

"You could do better." She couldn't help herself. Jake could have been anything, done anything. He had charm, looks, brains. He grinned, taking no offense.

"Want to share one of your brownies?"

"Sure. You know my sweet tooth can't say no." They sat at his old kitchen table and munched on the sweets that brought their mother halfway back into the room. It had been their parents' kitchen table once, heavy, wooden, never painted, scarred, water stained with big and small rings and cuts and dents from thousands of meals prepared and eaten on it, where their mother had cut up vegetables and pounded tough meat and kneaded dough and passed around the platters of steaming food. "Think you'll stay on at the service station for a while?"

"For a while. 'Til I get tired of it."

"When will it ever end?"

"You tell me. I'd be glad enough to get shut of this weary old world."

"I believe Jesus is coming soon. There are all the signs."

"Won't be too soon for me. I'm tired of waiting."

"What you waiting for, Jake?"

"For God to come, like you said. For God to come and show Himself and tell us what it's all about and do something, just do something."

"Do you believe in God, Jake? Sometimes I've wondered if you really believe in God at all."

"I wish to hell I didn't. I wish to hell I could believe there wasn't no God. Then I wouldn't blame him so much." He grinned, and Martha knew that their serious conversation was over. Jake had showed as much of himself as he was going to show in one afternoon. He unfolded the wrinkled faded blue denim shirt and put it on, covering himself up again and grinning with his good-natured, kind, piercing eyes that saw straight into other people but rarely let anyone look inside of him. His dark brown eyes, the windows of his soul, were made to see just one way, like those reflecting sunglasses that looked like mirrors on the outside.

THE TELEPHONE ringing beside their bed made Martha shake and twitch, even before she was fully awake. Frank had already answered and was speaking before she forced her eyes open. People said she had a gift for prophecy, and of course she knew what this call meant, but she'd had no inkling of its coming after they'd gone to bed. Jake had seemed to be in good spirits the last few days, maybe even cheerful, but in retrospect she remembered that cheerfulness could presage one of his drinking bouts, because his good humor was often a cover-up for how he was really feeling inside. The only questions now were where he was and who was calling, one of his neighbors or the sheriff.

Even before Frank finished talking on the phone, Martha had sat up on the side of the bed and begun putting on her hose. Frank would protest her going with him, but she would insist firmly. At first she'd let him go by himself, but that only led to more trouble later. Now she realized that he was talking to one of the deputy sheriffs. She thought it was easier when Jake was already in jail—fewer decisions to make—and felt guilty about the thought. It didn't necessarily mean that Jake had gotten into trouble away from home. His neighbors used to call them first, but some of his neighbors had grown weary of calling them and now called the sheriff's office directly. Martha couldn't really blame them, but she did appreciate the ones who still let them know before they called the law.

Frank had not yet gotten the receiver onto the cradle when she asked him, "What happened? Where is he?"

"In jail, of course."

"Was he at home, or did he get into trouble in town?"

"At home, I guess. The deputy said he was really out of his mind this time. You don't need to go."

"I'm coming with you." Frank didn't argue anymore. He didn't even answer her. He was worn out with all this. He had little enough patience for Jake even when there wasn't any crisis. Frank and Jake had been wary of each other, like animals of different species, even when they were boys.

They rode in silence in the car, as always when they were on a rescue mission for Jake. Frank didn't even turn on the radio to drown out the silence. There wouldn't have been anything to hear at three o'clock in the morning anyway. Some strands of Frank's straight black hair popped up in the back and on the sides. Usually every hair on

Frank's head would be in place when he went out in public, day or night. His mouth was turned down, and there were bags underneath his eyes. His whole face seemed to sag. Usually Frank was smiling. It wasn't a put-on smile. It didn't come and go. It was just part of his face, like his nose or his eyebrows. It was natural for Frank to smile. Maybe that's part of what made him such a good salesman. It took something unusual to wipe the smile off Frank's face, something bad and unpleasant, usually Jake.

"Mornin', Mr. Simmons, Miss Martha. I hate to call you out at this hour. But he's real bad this time." Tim, the deputy sheriff, was the one who had telephoned them.

Frank shook his weary, sad face. "Hard to believe he's any drunker than he was the last time."

"I'm not real sure he is. He's just crazier."

"Can we go back and see him?"

"Sure, Miss Martha. Come on this way."

He was pitiful. Martha took one look at him and knew that he belonged in the hospital, not in jail. "Frank, will you go pay the bond? Would you call us an ambulance, Tim? He needs to be in the hospital. I'll wait here with him." They obeyed her without any protests, just as the children had obeyed in her classroom when she taught school before she married Frank. When there was trouble, Martha deliberately took on her mantle of authority that no one ever seemed to question. As the men left the cellblock, she sat down on a bunk opposite where Jake lay huddled in a fetal position. Fortunately, there were not many prisoners in the county jail tonight, and Jake didn't have to share a cell. There was no one in the cell next door, and two cells down the corridor the prisoner was asleep and snoring loudly. The lights inside the cells had been turned off for the night, but there was enough illumination to see him clearly from the lighted bare bulbs inside their little wire cages in the corridor ceiling.

"Oooh."

"What is it, baby?"

"Oooh. The sun went black, and the stars come crashing into the ocean." He never opened his eyes and didn't seem to be aware that she was there with him.

"You're not making any sense, Jake. You've just had too much to drink."

"No, I ain't. The moon's gone away and never will come back. Never again, never see it again. Only God's left. Nothing else is real. We're not here. We're not real, just like old films, TV reruns of old black and white movies. Only God. That's all. Just God. Never see the moon no more." He became quiet and quit twitching. Martha remembered how she had twitched when the telephone was ringing, waking her up, almost exactly the same way.

When the ambulance driver and the paramedic rolled the gurney in, Jake didn't move until they tried to roll him off the bunk onto it. Even lowered, the top of it was a little higher than the bunk, and they had to lift him slightly by his shoulders and legs.

"Oooh. Where you taking me? To the judgment? To the judgment throne of God?"

"Just to the hospital, Jake. Take it easy now." Tim tried to hold Jake down on the gurney as they pulled the straps over his chest and he struggled to get up. "They're gonna help you feel some better. Lord, he's strong for such a little guy. Must be solid muscle."

"I saw it. I saw the terrible . . . It was awful. Oughtn't nobody ever have to look at it and open his eyes again."

"What'id you see, Jake?" The ambulance driver tried to get him centered on the gurney.

He moaned again. "It's all right, baby. Everything's going to be all right." Martha didn't have to ask what he had seen. She knew. She didn't want these men to ask him any more questions. "Let's just get him on out to the ambulance as quickly as we can." They obeyed her without any further comment. She'd donned her schoolmarmish mantle of authority again.

The next day Martha was sitting beside Jake's bed in the hospital reading a romance novel, the only thing she could read to pass the time and not have to think about. The hospital room was darker than the jail cell. The only light came from the tiny reading lamp behind the pullout chair that was provided for family members who stayed overnight to sleep on. Frank was adamantly opposed to her spending the night, and she hadn't protested. She didn't know what good she could have done during the night, but she got up early and came to the hospital before the orderlies started bringing the breakfast trays. It had been very quiet until the breakfast cart came rattling down the hall, banging trays, and the noise hadn't stopped since. She wanted to be there for the doctor's rounds, although she hadn't learned much. The doctor had said, "Same old, same old, Martha. He's going to kill himself if he doesn't quit drinking, but you already know that." Now it was about two o'clock in the afternoon, although it could just as well have been midnight or seven o'clock in the morning for all the difference it made in the darkened room. For the last couple of hours Jake was twitching less often, less violently, and sleeping more peacefully. He hadn't spoken since he came in, the nurses said, and not to her all day. Martha had eaten a few bites from his breakfast tray and almost all of his lunch. She didn't even try to wake him or ask him to eat. She knew it would be futile. She just waited. She didn't know quite what she was waiting for.

IT WAS HIS THIRD DAY in the hospital. "Jake, my pastor is here. Will you let him come in and speak to you?"

"If it will make you happy, Martha, but it's not gonna do me no good."

Martha's pastor was a round man. He had a round face and a round body. His nose was round. His ears were round. He had big round eyes behind round spectacles in translucent plastic frames that seemed outdated. Even his fingers seemed to extend and retract from the round balls of his hands like a cat's claws as he turned the thin crisp pages of his Bible, but she thought he had a good heart, even if his sermons were so dull that her mind often wandered.

In a Methodist church located in a small town you took whomever the bishop sent you and knew whoever came would be rotated out in four or five years and another pastor would arrive. Their present pastor, Brother Sams, was sincere in his faith and always meant well and did the best he could.

"Brother Jake, if you don't repent and turn to Jesus, you're going to lose your health and lose your very life in this world, but even worse than that you're going to lose your place in heaven with a sister who dearly loves you. It would grieve her precious heart not to have you with her singing praises around God's throne above. Now I'm telling it like it is. I'm not sparing anything just to be polite." Jake closed his eyes. "Brother Jake, I'd appreciate it if you opened your eyes and looked at me." Martha cringed. She knew that when Jake closed his eyes, he was listening with all his powers of concentration. He opened them and looked up at her pastor, smiling sweetly, with the blank expression that she knew meant he was tuning out every word that came from her pastor's mouth.

Brother Sams read some scriptures. During the twenty-third psalm Jake tuned in again briefly. Before Brother Sams left he took one of Jake's hands in one of his round red hands and took her hand in his other round red hand and prayed. Jake turned his face to the wall, so that Martha couldn't see his reaction. Perhaps it did some good. It was a sweet prayer, she thought; it seemed to come from the heart. When her pastor asked God to bless Jake and her and keep them in his loving care and protection, she felt Jake jerk and opened her eyes to see him twitch as he'd done when he first came into the hospital three days ago.

After Brother Sams left, Jake said, "He makes it all too simple, too easy. Just believe in Jesus. Trust in God, and everything will be all right. Hunky dory."

"Jake!"

"I'm sorry, Martha. I don't mean to say anything to hurt you. You're so good. Maybe God will give me a little credit on your account."

"You can't get to heaven on my coattails."

"I dunno, Martie. Your coattails are lots longer than you think they are." Jake grinned his irresistible grin and closed his eyes. Martha knew that he wasn't asleep. He was thinking very deeply within himself. Then with his eyes still closed, he began to talk, as if he were dictating a deposition into a machine, as if he had forgotten that she was still in the room. "They shall deliver you up to councils, and ye shall be brought before rulers and kings and sheriffs and judges and Methodist preachers. Yes, Lord, I've read your Bible, over and over, but I don't get any answers out of it. I never told you how Bucky died. Not all of it. Whenever we went into a village at first we tried to give something to the children. A stick of gum. A piece of candy or chocolate. Maybe just a picture post card or a piece of colored foil. They'd come running out. And that day they come running out, and we started toward them, and this one little boy reached inside his shirt and pulled out a grenade and hurled it straight at Buck. I saw it go off. I saw Buck's insides coming out red and white, and I remembered us skinny dipping in the lake and camping out and praying in church side by side. We'd been best friends since we was born, I guess. We enlisted together and went through basic together and shipped out together. I went over and held him together, what there was left of him to hold together, and heard him trying to breathe and gasp and stiffen up and go limp, and then, nothing, like he was a sack of manure." He was quiet for a long time, and Martha didn't say anything. "There ain't no easy answers. It's not that simple." He was quiet again, and his face contorted as if he were in great pain.

"Jake, you all right? Can I get you anything."

"You've heard all that before, but I haven't ever told you the other part." He seemed to go back inside himself and leave her, but she knew he was aware of her presence. Whatever it was he was trying to get out was the most difficult thing he had ever uttered. "Then we went to this other village, and this other boy come running out, exactly the same—same age, same clothes, same eyes, same chopped off hair, and he reached in his shirt the exact same way." Martha saw tears running down his cheeks, but he didn't seem to be crying. He was silent for what seemed to her a long time, while the tears rolled down his cheeks. He didn't try to wipe them off, and she decided it was better not to dab at him with her tissue. "And I shot him. Dead. He didn't have no grenade nor nothing. He probably just wanted a piece of gum . . . or chocolate."

"Jake, you couldn't have known."

He was silent for a very long time again. "I never picked him up and held him. You know what the Bible says, 'Brother shall betray brother to death, and the father shall betray the son; and children shall rise up against their parents, and shall cause them to be put to death.' Oh, I read my Bible, pastor. I read it good. I committed it to memory a long time ago. I saw the abomination of desolation, and I read and understand very well what it means. They thought I was crazy in the jail last week. You all thought I was crazy. It's the whole world that's crazy, not just me."

"Jake, God will forgive you. Then you can forgive yourself."

"Martha, if anybody else ever said that to me, I'd spit in his face, but you mean it. You love me. Maybe someday. I keep hoping. I keep waiting. But I doubt it."

"What would it take for you to believe that God will forgive you?"

"What would it take for me to forgive God? What kind of a god would let something like that happen? What kind of a god would let men plan a war like that? What kind of a god would let me do something like that?"

"You seemed all right when you first came home. You seemed like your old self, only older, wiser."

"Yeah, for a while I thought it was over with. That was over there, and over here it was completely different, a different world. I was a different man here at home. I'd left all that part of myself over there." He paused, as if he didn't know how to go on with his story.

Martha felt he need prompting, like one of her students who'd lost the train of thought when giving a book report. "Then Helen died."

"Yeah. Not just that she died. I learned to accept death. That's one thing I did learn over there, how death is a part of life. It's not easy, but you accept it and go on. But how she died, how she didn't have to die then. The insurance people wouldn't let her see a specialist until it got so bad, and when she did see a specialist, he said he could have saved her if she had just gotten to see him earlier. By then the cancer was all over her."

"But that's just human greed at work. You can't blame God."

"I blame God for creating people like that and letting them do things like that. I'd feel better about it if He had the guts to do things directly Hisself."

"Jake, please don't talk like that, even to me. Think how much it would hurt Mama."

"Mama! For Christ's sake, Martha! That was the final blow. Mama and Daddy burning up in that house, so burned that you couldn't even recognize who they were. It was as bad as anything I saw in 'Nam. Worse. Still, I could've accepted it. But when we found out that all those leading citizens had cheated on the building code and put in faulty wiring in the retirement apartments . . . shitfire! Ain't you still bitter, too?"

"Sure, I'm still bitter toward the people who built the apartments, but I'm not bitter toward God. I'll have to admit I just can't understand people like that."

"People like me, who'd shoot a little old boy in the belly. He hadn't hardly even started to grow hair around his privates."

"You were scared. You didn't understand."

"I was not scared. I was angry, and I did understand. Don't you give me easy answers. Don't you make it too simple like your preacher man, Sis. You know better. Don't you be seduced by false Christs and false prophets with their signs and wonders. You know better than that."

"Jake, there's nothing I can say to you except I love you."

"That's the damned trouble. Your long loving coattails. That's why I keep hanging in there. 'Wait, watch, for ye know not the hour when the master is coming.' See, Sis, I know my Bible too well. I mock it, and it mocks me."

FRANK PULLED his fingers from his temples through his fine black hair to the back. Martha knew from the familiar habit that he was preoccupied about something, and she could guess it was about Jake. "What is it, hon?"

"Jake."

"I figured."

"At the meeting they were talking about an intervention." Frank and Martha had begun attending an Al-Anon group after Jake's latest binge. Frank had all the enthusiasm and ignorance of a new convert, who believed the perfect solution to their problems lay at hand. "When do you think we ought to try it?"

Martha warned herself to be cautious. If Frank thought she was summarily dismissing his plan, they would all pay the price for his disappointment for weeks to come. "I dunno, hon. They say you get together all these people that are important—family, friends, bosses, preachers, girlfriends—but who's Jake got besides us? He's got no other family. He doesn't have a church or a girlfriend. He hasn't had a boss in years that he respected or that cared anything about him. And his friends . . ."

" . . . are all drunks, too. But we've got to do something. We can't just let him keep on like this. Maybe we should do an intervention, just the two of us, you and me. The people at the meeting could tell us how."

Martha moved around some pots on the range that didn't need moving to give herself a few moments to think about what to say. "How many times have we already talked to him. What would be different now?"

"Maybe we've learned something new to say, from going to the meetings."

"Maybe." Then an idea occurred to her, and she felt some of the same kind of enthusiasm for it that Frank had expressed for the intervention. "You know what would be different? We've talked to him, and I've talked to him, but you've never talked to him by yourself."

Frank stopped pulling his fingers through his hair. He looked terrified. "You mean just me? All by myself?"

"He might listen to what you have to say if I wasn't around. You always accuse me of protecting him, and maybe I do, and as you said, you've learned some new things lately."

"Jake would never listen to me. We're too different. We've never gotten along."

Martha set the pots down finally and sat at the kitchen table across from Frank. It was a risk facing him and talking so directly to him that he might rebuke her, but it seemed time to take some kind of risk. "That's just not so. Of course you're different. You do things in different ways, but there are a lot of ways you're more alike than you are different. I think that's why I love you both so much. When we were in school, neither one of you could stand to see children bullied or taken advantage of. You're both still that way. When there was a wrong or injustice, Jake would get into a fist fight and you'd start a petition." Frank smiled, and Martha breathed a sigh of relief. His smile was broad, showing all his teeth, like silent laughter, not like Jake's sheepish grin.

"Well, you got that about right."

"Whenever people are mistreated, you and Jake are about the only people I've ever known who just have to do something about it." Martha thought of all the good causes Frank sent money to—from starving children to refugees to Indian missions to projects that helped women start businesses in Central America. She didn't even know half the list of things. Sometimes she resented all the money he spent, in addition to their tithe to the church—and it was a full 10 percent tithe—but his generosity was what she most loved and admired about Frank. "It's what I love about you both."

"Not that it ever changes things." What Martha most disliked was Frank's reading the newspaper and newsmagazines. When the poverty rate got worse or there were reports of more starving children, he became bitter and cynical, as if his concerns and his donations should have changed the world.

"But you try."

"And Jake tries, too, I suppose. When somebody was treated unfairly, he'd go out and pick a fight with the bully, like you said, and then go out and get drunk when nothing changed, whether he got whooped or whooped somebody's ass." Martha knew how much Frank had always secretly admired Jake, and she could see in his eyes now that he recognized his admiration, almost envy. "Win or lose, he'll go and get drunk, and I . . ." It was a rare moment of self-understanding for Frank, and Martha wouldn't touch it with a ten foot pole. He began pulling his long slender fingers through his fine black hair again, like combs through glistening waves of silk. "I think I'll do it. I'll try it. But I've got to think about it a while so I can try and do it right."

Martha began weeping, she loved him so much, and Frank got up and came around the table and put his arm around her and kissed her, first on the forehead and then full on the mouth.

Day after day Martha felt an overwhelming happiness and joy. She woke up every morning singing inside her head and went to sleep every night humming like a contented baby who'd just finished nursing. It was all she could do to keep from giggling, the way she had giggled when Frank had first asked her out in high school and later as she told her girlfriends about their dates. (Her girlfriends couldn't believe at first that one of the best looking, most popular boys in school would want to date Martha, as ordinary looking as she was. They couldn't believe it would last. She could hardly believe it herself. She still sometimes couldn't believe it would last.) Now there was no one to tell, and she couldn't put Jake's new lease on life into so many words. Of course, she made no secret that Jake had gone into treatment and was attending the AA meetings as faithfully as she and Frank had gone to Wednesday evening prayer meetings and worship services in the morning and at night every Sunday all their married life; she was not privy, however, to the secrets that Jake and Frank seemed to keep between the two of them.

She was afraid Jake might lose his sobriety, but in her heart she felt that it was solid and sure. Even if he fell off the wagon and drank again—a possibility he often acknowledged with one of his slogans from AA, "one day at a time"—he was a changed person and could never again become the person that he had been before.

There was never an open AA function that Frank did not attend with Jake to show his support. Martha would have given a pretty penny to know just what Frank had said to Jake at his "intervention," but it was one of their secrets and a secret that she knew would never be revealed to her. Jake had gone into a treatment program almost immediately after they'd talked. He gave up his work at the filling station, and Frank paid all the cost for the treatment program, although Jake had now repaid them every cent. Frank hadn't wanted to take Jake's money, he was so happy about Jake's reformation and his part in it, but at that point she had intervened herself with Frank and told him they would have to take Jake's money for the sake of his pride.

Jake's testimony — six months later

When Jake woke up thirsty sometime after one o'clock in the morning and noticed that the porch light was still on, he stuck his head into the front room and saw the little boudoir lamp of his mother's also burning. (She'd always insisted on calling it a "bourdoir lamp." It used to sit on her dresser which was now in Martha's guest bedroom, but he'd inherited the lamp and used it in his front room as something like a night light.) The sofa bed hadn't been pulled out, so he knew that Lien hadn't come in. Maybe she would arrive later, after one of her tricks. Maybe she wouldn't stop by at all tonight.

For the past several weeks he'd left the front door unlocked for her, but in this neighborhood leaving your front door open was an invitation to trouble. Although the sorry characters around here were afraid of him, other scoundrels that came looking for drugs or sex on the street might not know his reputation as a bad dude. He'd told her to ring the bell and wake him up and he'd let her inside, that he'd go back to sleep right away—he had no trouble sleeping, but she was shy and timid about disturbing him. When she'd told him that this was the only place she felt safe, with tears streaming down her thin little face, he'd given her a key and told her to come and go as she pleased. In those months that she'd crashed here, she'd never taken anything of his. So far as he could tell, she'd never even rummaged through any of his things. She would fold up her bed and slip out in the morning, so he might not have even known that she'd been here, except for the flower she'd leave on the kitchen table or a note or sketch, always signed with a smiley face. Her drawings were good enough to frame and put up on the wall. She was a talented artist, Jake thought, although he didn't really know anything about art. She'd always left something to thank him.

He'd told her if she ever brought a man in here, he'd throw her out for good, and when she'd cried, he felt terrible and put his arms around her; she'd sobbed even harder and muttered, "I'd never do that" in between her gasps for breath.

A year or more ago, sometimes on weekends and early in the evening before she went out on the street, they'd talked. It was hard to say exactly when they'd spoken the first time. He'd seen her on the street when he was working on his car or mowing the front yard and especially at night sitting on the porch smoking and drinking a beer. (He'd never done his hard drinking outside. Whenever he started on a bottle of whiskey, he'd open it inside and finish it inside before the night was out.) He'd smile and wave at her, and she'd smile back. Most of the other neighbors turned away from her, knowing what she was doing. He knew, too, but it wasn't his place to judge her. Somehow she figured out that his smiles and waves weren't a response to her come-ons for business.

One cold November night after he'd quit drinking and started going to AA three or four times a week, he'd told her she needed to put something on her bare legs and belly or she was going to freeze.

"You want to put your legs and belly around me and cover me up and keep me warm?"

"No, I don't care for you that way."

"How do you care for me then?"

"Just as a friend."

She'd looked so tired and scared and cold that he'd asked her to come inside, and she'd fallen asleep on the couch for a couple of hours. Then they started teasing back and forth more often, and as they chatted more often and a little longer each time, she began to trust him and say what she really meant and even a little about how she felt.

Lien turned the key in the lock and opened the door while Jake was standing there in the front room in the dark. "Why do you do this? You're too good for this kind of life." She jumped like a rabbit hearing a gunshot.

"You scared the life outa me. I need the money, that's why."

"Need it for what? You got a job." She worked at the Dairy Queen during the day. Sometimes Jake would stop after work for a milkshake and tease her.

"It's not enough. I need more to get away."

"Get away from what?"

For some reason Lien decided to open up that night as it drew on toward two o'clock in the morning, and she told Jake everything. After her father died, her mother had married a black man in Birmingham. He was an educated black man who made a lot of money. Maybe he thought that having a wife from Asia made him special. Lien didn't think he loved her mother all that much. He seemed to have bought them, like the new cars and the fancy house with the marble entrace and the swimming pool and the brick driveway and the three car garage, to show off to the neighbors.

Lien was only thirteen when he began to have sex with her. She said it wasn't rape, that he'd talked her into it. Jake would have called it rape, and he clenched his fists as she told him about it. After he'd shot that boy in 'Nam, he'd never had the impulse to hurt anybody again, in spite of his reputation in the neighborhood, and he'd learned how to put on a good bluff from the days he really was a bad dude, but he thought if he ever met her stepfather, somebody would have to hold him down to keep him from beating the crap of out him. Lien said she liked sex. She said she'd liked the sex even with her stepfather. It was other things she didn't like about him, and Jake kept his mouth shut and let her talk. He knew from people nagging him about his drinking that arguing with her wouldn't do any good. Someday something

would happen that would give her the idea to change. Someone would
say something; maybe even he would say just the right thing at just the
right time. Meanwhile, he just listened, and she told him that whenever
she went back to Birmingham to visit her mother, she still had sex with
her stepfather. Jake knew she probably said it just to get a rise out of
him, although he stayed quiet. When he clenched his teeth and made
a tight fist, he could see a little shameful look on her face, even while
she kept on talking in that proud, contrary way of hers, like she was
bragging to him about what a bad girl she was.

Lien probably didn't expect Jake to come home early enough the next
evening from Martha and Frank's house, where he usually had supper,
to find her sitting in the dark when he switched on the overhead light,
and he surely didn't expect to see her at this early hour of the night,
curled up in the big overstuffed, scratchy red chair that had been in
his folks' living room along with the matching sofabed before they'd
moved to that damned apartment. (After they'd moved to the apartment, Martha had called and told him what she wanted from their
family's house and asked what he wanted and said she would sell the
rest. When he'd told her he wanted the red chair and sofa, she'd said
they weren't worth anything and weren't worth storing, and he'd told
her to go ahead and sell them then, that he didn't care all that much
about them, but when he got back to town after the war, he found that
Martha, being Martha, had stored them for him.) Lien looked as small
now as he'd felt almost thirty years ago curled up in that chair. It had
seemed to be the safest place in the world to him, too, back then, and
a comforting place when he was sad and lonely.

"Oh!"

Jake laughed. "I scared you about as bad tonight as I scared you
early this morning, I reckin. Guess neither one of us expected to see
each other this time of the evening. You feeling bad? Sick?"

Lien shook her head. "Not sick."

"Just got the Thursday night blues?" (She smiled faintly, and Jake
sat down and wondered whether to talk or not.) "You want company

or just want to be by yourself?"

Lien shrugged. Jake waited a minute to figure out what she meant or whether she'd give him any other signal, and then he stretched over his head and turned off the ceiling light and then reached across the sofa and turned on the boudoir lamp. He knew she wouldn't think he was trying to come on to her. He figured she might tell him what was bothering her if the room wasn't too bright.

"Why are you being so nice to me?"

"I like being nice to people."

"You're not always nice to people."

"Yeah?"

"And I'm a bad person. You're such a good person."

"The hell you say!"

"You've never done anything really bad."

"Just gone on drunks and lost all my jobs and run off all my friends, the decent ones."

"I mean something really bad."

Jake didn't know what to say next. He wondered if this was his chance to say something that might make her want to change. "I killed somebody once. A little boy. In Viet Nam, where you come from."

Lien looked at him without any expression on her face; it was like she hadn't understood what he'd said, like what he'd said didn't have any meaning to her. "Is that why you took me in then? To make up for what you did?"

"No. I don't think so. I ain't sure."

"Is that what made you drink? Remembering how you killed a boy?"

"That was a big part of it, I think. Not all of it."

"Was he a soldier in the war?"

"No. He was just a little boy, about ten or twelve years old prob'ly. I thought he was gonna throw a bomb or something at me, but he didn't have no weapons at all on him."

"That's awful."

"Yeah."

"What made you quit drinking?"

"I dunno, exactly. I figured I had to quit hurting the people what cared about me and loved me, and I had to quit hurting myself. It wasn't doing no good."

"Do you love me, Jake?"

"Yeah. I do." He hoped she wouldn't get the wrong idea now.

"Enough to make me quit fucking men for money?"

He had to take the risk. "Yeah."

"Well, maybe I think about it then. I want to go to sleep now, if you don't mind."

Thank the good Lord she hadn't asked him to come to bed with her. She seemed to understand what he'd been trying to get at. Maybe he'd been able to say the right thing at the right time after all.

"Yeah. Sure. Good night."

He grinned what he knew was the sheepish grin that seemed to make people feel better a lot of times. Lien smiled back at him, and he thought, 'She's gonna be all right. She's really gonna be all right now.' When he crawled into bed in his undershorts and undervest, the front room was completely dark, not even the glow from the boudoir lamp showed under the door. For a man who thought that he had never any trouble falling asleep, he lay awake for several hours, and for a man who said he didn't believe in God, he found himself saying something like a prayer of thanks.

Habitual Rituals

Nothing could be accomplished on the morning once a month when the altar guild members gathered to polish brass and silver. With all their chatter and laughter it was impossible to write a sermon; trapped in my office, even reading was difficult with the hubbub next door. I was aggravated when I should have been grateful for the time and effort they contributed to St. Mary Magdalene. The church architect who placed the kitchen and sacristy next to the rector's study must have been an idiot. Of course, it was necessary to be there and not run down to the post office or even make a hospital call, unless there was an emergency, in case they needed to ask me something about schedules or the set up for services during the month.

Edna knocked before she came in but entered before I replied—that was unusual. Then she sat down on the edge of the chair, not leaning back, before I could say, 'Please sit down'—that was even more unusual. Only Edna could look elegant in an apron stained with brass and silver polish. "Gwaltney, I wanted to let you know that Sam and I will be gone for a few weeks."

"You're not going to be away for Holy Week and Easter, are you?" My aggravation was peaking toward nasty belligerence. I couldn't get through the end of Lent without Edna around to corral the altar guild and acolytes and lay readers. She was like a full-time unpaid member of the staff.

"I'm not sure. We hope to be back."

"Where're you headed this time? France or Italy?" Sam and Edna made annual jaunts to Paris or Naples or Florence or Rome, always to either France or Italy, sometimes even twice a year.

"Baltimore."

"What the hell's in Baltimore?"

"Johns Hopkins. The doctors here are perfectly capable, but you know Sam. He won't let any stone be left unturned. Just in case. I have cancer. They say it's serious—terminal."

For what seemed an eternity I couldn't speak. Then I said, "Edna," and after another long pause, "I'm so sorry."

"I know, Gwaltney. Sam's going to need you and Barbara a lot." Then she said, almost as an afterthought, "I will, too."

"What can I do?"

"Right now all we need are your prayers. Later . . . I'll let you know. We're not telling people about it just yet. You can tell Barbara, of course, but please keep it confidential. I'm not ready to talk about it—even with you. Let me get back to polishing the brass, and we'll talk later."

"At least let me give you a hug and a blessing."

"That would be nice." She received my hug and brief prayer as she always did, stiffly, with a dignified smile, without any tears or maudlin display of self-pity.

After she left I stared at the camellias in the vase in front of me and wondered who would keep flowers on my desk every day. What a horrible, selfish thought! In the twenty-seven years that I'd been the Rector of St. Mary Magdalene there had hardly been a day when fresh flowers did not grace my study. I'd arrived at this parish fresh out of seminary—in the old days when candidates went straight from college to seminary to ordination—at the ripe age of twenty-five. Barbara and I were expecting our first child and also expecting to remain at the little church for no more than a couple or three years. The friendship and support of Sam and Edna were among the reasons we stayed on year after year. In the meantime the little parish grew into a big parish with a full-time staff of seven and young associate priests who came and went, but the flowers on my desk provided continuity and a sense of stability as well as beauty and encouragement. Usually the flowers came from Edna's extensive garden, which had blossoms nine or ten months out of the year. Camellias gave way to daffodils then tulips then irises then peonies then roses until the first freeze.

When Sam and Edna had made their first trip to France a few months after my arrival, I'd thought my desk would be bereft of flowers, but Edna had arranged for one of the younger altar guild members to go over to Edna's garden after driving her children to school and snip stems of roses and arrange them before I arrived each morning. When she was in town Edna brought flowers by on her way to the gym long before I made it to the office. Only a dozen or so times over the years did I have an emergency that brought me to the church early enough to catch her putting flowers into a vase, dressed in her work-out clothes.

After Sam and Edna had left for a winter vacation in Italy just after my first decade anniversary at St. Mary Magdalene, when all the gardens in town were brown, even Edna's, I'd thought the flowers would be forgotten. Sure enough, when I arrived at my office a couple of days after their departure, I saw the wilting blossoms that Edna had deposited the day before their flight, but around ten o'clock the florist had come with a new bud vase and returned to replenish it until Edna and Sam came home. She never liked carnations. She said they reminded her of funerals, and when she discovered upon returning that the florist had put carnations on my desk, she became irate. It was the only time I ever heard her raise her voice and curse, and when I laughed, she joined in the laughter at herself.

Soon the flowers on my desk would be no more. I would miss many, many other things without Edna, but my loss would be miniscule compared to Sam's. How would Sam survive without Edna?

How could I tell Barbara? Edna was like a mother and a sister and a best friend all combined for her. And what about my children? They would be devastated. When all the girls Brittainy's age were learning to swim, my daughter was terrified of the water, and I assumed the role of a controlling, demanding, frustrated, angry, anxious father—I didn't usually behave that way, I thought. Edna had told me to go away, "Just leave, Gwaltney." Then she cajoled Brittainy to dunk her face and head and lift her legs and feel the support and security of the water holding her. Soon Brittainy was swimming like a duck, and a decade or so later Edna and Sam arranged for her to work as a summer lifeguard at the country club. Brittainy often said that those summers at the country club pool were the happiest times of her life.

When Aidan reached the teenage phase of non-communication with his parents, he and all his buddies felt comfortable hanging out for hours with Sam and Edna at their pool. Even though he was ashamed to be seen with us, he confided all his fears and hopes to his godparents, who lovingly restored him to our care after a couple of years of adolescent prodigality.

My most painful thoughts were focused on Sam. How could I possibly minister to Sam? It would be one of the greatest challenges of my priesthood. I couldn't even imagine Sam without Edna. As St. Mary Magdalene grew, the small clinic where Sam was chief of staff grew into a large regional medical center, and the growth of one had much to do with the growth of the other. The reputation of Sam and the hospital brought many new families to the area. Sam worked hard and effectively, but he always made time for Edna and for their friends and for the church.

Sam and Edna could not have children. She had a niece and a nephew who had lived with them for several years at a time when their parents were having problems with drugs and financial fraud. Sam and Edna had paid for their college educations. Perhaps the responsibility for her niece and nephew at a critical period in their lives prevented Edna and Sam from considering adoption. I once raised the question of why they hadn't adopted children and was rebuffed. It was the only subject I ever broached that met a forbidden entrance into their privacy. They were godparents, however, not only to our children but also to scores of other children in town.

The attention they paid to their godchildren typified how they functioned as a couple. Each of their godchildren was invited to dinner on a date close to their birthdays but never on the actual day, so as not to conflict with their families' and school friends' celebrations. Their birthday gifts were always thoughtful and imaginative and appropriate for each particular child. The menu was always carefully designed with the same personal consideration. Other special honors and milestones followed a similar ritual. Edna did all the preparation and selected the gifts, but Sam was always present for the event. Sam was a hugger of both girls and boys, regardless of their age, and his emotional warmth wrapped Edna's brilliant offerings in a perfect package. Children often talked about Dr. Sam and Miss Edna, rarely if ever speaking of them separately, just as adults spoke of Sam and Edna as if they were two avatars of the same person.

When I glanced down at my watch and was startled to see that I'd spent an hour musing on how Edna's death would affect many people far and wide, I realized that I'd given no attention to how Edna herself might feel. In all the years I'd known her, Edna had deflected attention away from herself and toward others. Would it be the same now that she was dying? Would that be what she wanted and needed or only the habitual response she had cultivated in us?

SAM AND EDNA returned to town on (what we used to call) Passion Sunday. Edna was too weak to attend services at the church, but she supervised the altar guild by telephone from her home and covered every detail. Holy Week and Easter services proceeded flawlessly according to her directions. I brought her communion on Maundy Thursday and again on Easter afternoon. She looked gaunt on Thursday night and wore a robe. I sensed death hovering around her, as I'd often felt its ominous immanence when I visited other dying parishioners. By Easter she was impeccably dressed and stretched out on a sofa with makeup covering her pallor in a way that reminded me how the faces of corpses were painted as they lay in their caskets during wakes at the funeral home.

On Maundy Thursday there had been a few roses in bud vases on her piano much like those she had put on the altar over the years. "They should look like flowers on the kitchen table for a family supper," she'd told the new members of the altar guild every year. "It's like a family supper that we're remembering." On Easter afternoon the floral arrangements around the living room were more elaborate but still appropriate for a home rather than for the chancel of a church. "Was Edna up to arranging the flowers?" I asked Sam as he let me out the front door.

"Oh, no. She directed me doing them. Very exactly, as you might imagine."

"How is she, Sam?"

"The doctors at Johns Hopkins were very encouraging. It's a new medication, still being tested. We'll just have to wait and see. It'll take some time to be effective."

Neither of them were ready to talk yet. 'Or were they just not willing to talk to me?' I wondered in a paranoid moment.

By Pentecost Edna was looking well and back at the church undertaking almost all of her usual tasks. Sam told me that the regime seemed to be working and she was in remission. They wanted to live normally and not think or talk about "dire outcomes," as he put it. In midsummer they planned to make their annual trip to Europe. When Sam told me about the plans for Provence, I realized that he was making arrangements for travel that would be easier for Edna than they had chosen on previous trips, but the great surprise was his doing the planning and making the arrangements rather than Edna. He'd suggested going to Switzerland for a change, where it would be cool, but Edna didn't want to alter their customary rituals that much.

In the early fall Edna oversaw the dinner for the bishop's visit as usual. They invited the teenagers in the confirmation class to come to their home for a swim and dinner, as they did every year, but Edna did allow some of the meal to be catered; she didn't do all the cooking herself. "She's not quite completely herself yet," Sam told me, "but we're still very encouraged. She should be back to normal soon."

By mid-September Edna took a sudden turn for the worse. The experimental medicine had run its course and done all it could do for her. The remission was over. It would be only a matter of time. She was dying. Annointing of the sick now always accompanied the reserved communion that I brought her every week. Sam stopped by my office at least a couple of times a week, but all he ever said was a hundred variations of "I don't know what I'm going to do without her." Edna talked comfortably and easily about her impending death but her only other commentary was a hundred variations of "Take care of Sam." She put all of her affairs in order. She named her replacement on the altar guild and all her committees and offices. Technically it was my prerogative to make those assignments, but of course I deferred to her.

As September drew to a close I was faced with a dilemma. Our family vacation was planned for the last two weeks of October. We were gong to the cabin in Vermont that we'd rented when our children were teenagers. It would be the last vacation for just the four of us because Brittainy was to be married the following spring. I approached Sam about canceling or deferring my vacation.

"You can't do that, Gwaltney. How many times as Senior Warden have I heard you say, 'We can't wait for people to die'? When Edna's time comes, I'll call you, and if it's possible, I hope you can come back for her funeral."

"Of course, I will."

During the next couple of weeks Edna seemed to stabilize or at least not become any worse. It appeared she had been given another respite, another minor remission, although this time she was living in a much diminished state. And so we left for Vermont on October 14.

I called Sam at least every other day, and when I hung up the phone on the Saturday of our first weekend away, Barbara asked, "How's Edna doing."

"She's dying." That seemed to break the denial at least within our family. One by one we reminisced about our favorite memories and anecdotes.

Aidan told us how he'd called Edna after he'd had his first car wreck, when he was sixteen, because he knew that Edna wouldn't scream at him, as I would, or act bewildered, as Sam would, or dissolve in anxiety about his well-being, as Barbara would. Then Barbara talked about the secrets she'd shared with Edna over the years and held us in shocked amazement as she revealed some of them to us for the first time, especially the occasions when she'd slipped away by herself to Sam and Edna's beach house because she felt compelled to get away from her family and the church and had told us she was going to visit her mother. Brittainy began to relate some of her intimate encounters with Edna, but she broke down in the middle of talking about them.

"How can I get married without Edna there to arrange everything? It will be a disaster."

"We'll manage." Barbara hugged her but glanced over at me with eyes that wondered just how we would manage, whether it really would be a disaster without Edna's direction.

"We keep wondering how we'll get along without Edna and remembering all that she's done for us, but I keep thinking about what we can do for her." It was a query that had preoccupied me for the last several weeks. Edna seemed so self-sufficient, even as she faced her death, that she didn't seem to need anything from any of us, but the answer came in a telephone call just past sunset on Sunday.

"Gwaltney, I'd promised myself I wouldn't call you until it was all over, but Edna's in a bad way. She says she can't die until she talks to you. She says she has to make her confession, although I can't imagine what she would have to confess. She says she can't talk to anybody but you. James"—our latest young priest associate—"has been wonderful, but . . ."

"I'll be there tomorrow. As soon as I can get a plane out of here."

"I hate to ask you . . ."

"Thank God you did. Maybe I can finally do something for Edna . . . and you."

"You've done plenty for me, Gwaltney, but I know what you mean. It's hard to do anything for Edna. If you can't get a flight, call me, and I'll send a charter up there to bring you down."

"I will." I considered not even calling for a reservation on an airline, so that Sam could participate in doing something for Edna by chartering a plane, but my sense of the stewardship of expenses won out, and I had no difficulty getting an early flight home the next morning.

Edna had been taken to the hospital. Sam had kept her at home as long as possible, but even with nurses around the clock and his medical skills, she finally needed to be where she could receive more care. When Sam and I entered the darkened room, her nephew was holding her hand on one side of the bed, and her niece was holding her other hand on the other side of the bed. Edna rasped, "You all go out in the hall for a minute so I can talk with Gwaltney." As they had always done, they obeyed her immediately without question. "Gwaltney, I want to make my confession."

"Formally or just conversationally?"

"By the book."

The room was too dark to read the words from *The Book of Common Prayer*, but I'd memorized the substance of "The Reconciliation of a Penitent" after repeating it over and over, especially during Lent.

"Edna, you begin by saying 'Bless me, for I have sinned.'"

"Bless me for I have sinned."

"'The Lord be in your heart and upon your lips that you may truly and humbly confess your sins: In the Name of the Father, and of the Son, and of the Holy Spirit. Amen.' Now you say after me . . ." And Edna repeated the phrases, like brides and grooms do in making their vows on their wedding day. "'I confess to Almighty God . . . to his Church, and to you . . . that I have sinned by my own fault in thought, word and deed . . . in things done and left undone . . . especially.' Now Edna, you say whatever it is you want to confess."

She sighed twice before she began and then paused. Her voice was faint and yet firm and resolute. "I smoked cigarettes. Almost every week. Not many. Four or five a month probably. I started in college, and I never quit. I kept it a secret from my parents. They would have been mortified. I was addicted. I never told Sam. I used mouthwash and mints. He must never know. He would be devastated." She was silent, and I waited a long time for her to continue.

"Is that all?"

"That's enough."

"Then you say after me, 'For these and all other sins which I cannot now remember . . . I am truly sorry . . . I pray God to have mercy on me . . . I firmly intend amendment of life.'"

"Gwaltney, that's ridiculous. I'll be dead in a little while."

"I know. You said you wanted it by the book."

"What are the words again?"

"'I firmly intend amendment of life . . . and I humbly beg forgiveness of God and his Church . . . and ask your counsel . . . direction . . . and absolution . . .'"

"Edna, you've lived a good and holy life and blessed many, many people. Smoking. It's not such a terrible thing."

"It is to me. It's a betrayal."

I pronounced the absolution. "The Lord has put away your sins."

Without prompting, she responded, "Thanks be to God."

"Abide in peace, and pray for me, a sinner."

"I will, Gwaltney. You can count on it. Thanks. Call the family back in, if you don't mind. I'm ready now."

Within an hour Edna's breathing became shallow. She moved her lips, but we couldn't hear her words. As if with the last fragment of her strength, with great exertion, she moved her hand across the surface of the bed and tugged at her niece's sleeve. Julia bowed her ear close to Edna's lips to hear her whispers.

"She says to raise the shade enough for us to read the litany."

"'God the Father, Have mercy on your servant. God the Son, have mercy on your servant. God the Holy Spirit, have mercy on your servant. Holy Trinity, one God, have mercy on your servant. From all evil, from all sin, from all tribulation, Good Lord, deliver her.'"

The setting sun dropped low enough below the window shade to fill the room with a golden glow, but the light seemed to be coming from Edna's body, as if she were radiating an ethereal luminescence.

Before we finished the litany, Sam stopped reading and interrupted us. "She's dead." He was aware as a doctor, as her beloved husband. "She's at peace." His voice was quiet, almost as soft as Edna's had been when she made her confession, but he was not weeping. Sam was at peace, too. Even Julia's and Jerry's tears had dried.

"Shall we finish, Sam, or stop here?"

"Let's finish, by all means. That's what Edna wanted."

I anointed Edna's body and we said the Lord's Prayer together.

"'Deliver your servant, Edna, O Sovereign Lord Christ, from all evil, and set her free from every bond, that she may rest with all your saints in the eternal habitations, where with the Father and the Holy Spirit you live and reign, one God, for ever and ever. Amen.'"

EDNA'S FUNERAL was exactly as she had planned it, down to the last detail, and it was beautiful, but the reception after the service veered away from her explicit directions. The flowers on the altar inside the church looked exactly as if Edna had arranged them herself with absolute balance and symmetry: one red rose on the left, one red rose on the right, one white rose beside the red rose on the left, one white rose beside the red rose on the left, a fern perfectly snipped to exactly the same height behind the roses on the left and the right and so on and so on. The arrangements the altar guild placed in the parish hall for the reception, however, were in varying shapes and forms, some of them looking almost Japanese in influence. Edna had dictated that the food would be catered, but the women of the parish prepared all of Edna's famous recipes, which she had believed were absolute secrets, but which they had figured out years ago, even though no one had ever dared to serve them in public during her lifetime.

"Edna would have been pleased," I thought. "Edna would have been amused. Edna would have been delighted." I could almost hear her deep-throated, distinctive chuckle.

Sam came over to thank me for the service, to thank me for all I'd done for Edna and him during her final illness, to thank me for our years of friendship, and I let him go on and on thanking me rather than reciprocating with my thanks for all that Sam and Edna had done and given to bless me and my family, because letting Sam express his gratitude without diminishing it with my own gratitude was my gift to him. "It's so ironic, Gwaltney, that Edna should die from lung cancer, when she never smoked a cigarette in her life."

"It's quite ironic indeed."

Miss Evelyn's Legacy

Don't tell me it's my day for goin' to that old witch's lair again already."

"Birdy, you should be ashamed of yourself talking like that about Miss Evelyn."

"I didn't use the 'b' word, even though it fits her better."

"You know she's not that bad. You're just being outrageous . . . unless you really do need to swap out with somebody."

"Hell no, Marian. You must spend half your life scheduling her helpers. When's the old biddy goin' to her reward? She must be a hundred and ten by now."

"Birdy, I don't have time to listen to your nonsense. I gotta go."

"Don't worry; I'll be there at ten o'clock Tuesday morning."

"Nine o'clock, Birdy."

"I know. I'm just playin' with you. You know I love you. Don't run yourself ragged, you hear. Come on down to the club Wednesday, and I'll treat you to lunch."

"I'll try."

"You do it. You need a day off to have some fun."

"I said I'd try."

"I'm expecting you. Take care of yourself. I mean it."

"Bye now, Birdy."

"Bye, sweet thing."

Marian hung up the phone. She could picture Robin Ethridge Smith in her frilly lace negligee, smoking an unfiltered cigarette in that strange wire contraption she'd invented to keep from getting tobacco stains on her fingers. Marian wondered if her objections to caring for Miss Evelyn originated in not being able to smoke while attending her. About a third of the people in town called Birdy "Mrs. Ethridge-Smith." The second third called her "Robin," and the final third "Miss Robin."

Only a dozen or so women were allowed to call Robin "Birdy." Marian was not sure it was a favor to be included in that select company. The marriage of Robin Byrd Ethridge to Harvey Ellison Smith III united the two wealthiest clans in this part of the state. It had been celebrated before Marian moved here, and of course it happened down in the city where both families lived, but everyone in the northern half of the state had heard about it, like a royal wedding.

The Ethridge-Smiths had moved here long after Miss Evelyn made her dramatic bequest, when it was still a poor farming community, just as the gated development of million dollar homes began to appear like the mirage of Camelot in the middle of a cow pasture, when the little Presbyterian Church was debating whether to close its doors and sell the property. The Ethridge-Smiths were Presbyterians. When they joined the little church, all their rich neighbors followed them. They had expected to expend money and efforts to revitalize the place. They hadn't expected to inherit the sacred promise that had been made to Miss Evelyn.

Marian dreaded the next call most of all. Marian herself took Mondays to check on how things had gone during the weekend and see what was needed for the week ahead. Originally there had been enough volunteers so that each woman had to serve only one day a month, but as more and more women took jobs outside the home she had to ask them to work two days a month, and now the five of them served every weekday. No one had expected Miss Evelyn to live well into her nineties and remain in such good health that she could stay in her own home with their help and not be put in the nursing home. The women with salaried jobs took Saturdays and Sundays and also came on weekday evenings to put Miss Evelyn to bed. Fortunately, Marian still found enough volunteers to need them only once a month; their Saturday and Sunday obligations rotated so that they came up only twice during the year on weekends. Working out the schedules and dealing with emergency swaps were difficult, but she disliked the weekly telephone reminders more, especially the call to Peggy.

Peggy had grown up in the cotton mill village and married the boy

who lived next door to her. No one had expected his chicken processing plant to grow into one of the biggest industries in the state. They
were smart, hard working, calculating, and as Birdy put it, "utterly
nouveau riche."

Peggy and Harold probably left the Baptist Church and joined the
Presbyterian Church in order to associate with Harvey and Birdy, but
in all fairness to them they weren't the only ones who made a similar
move for the same reason. Birdy took Peggy under her wing. She had
asked Peggy to call her "Birdy"—an act akin in this little town to being knighted by the queen. Only Birdy could have persuaded Peggy
to stop wearing her emerald and diamond bracelet and fur stole and
spike heel shoes to the grocery store and not only kept her friendship
but also won her unfailing devotion.

"Peggy? Just checking to be sure you're ready for your duties with
Miss Evelyn Wednesday."

"Yeah. I'll be there as usual, but Marian, how long is this gonna
go on? She'd be a whole lot better off in the nursing home, you know.
It's not like the church couldn't afford to pay for it. We're not the poor
little country church we were when this all started."

"I know, Peggy, but we did make a promise . . ." 'I know all too well,'
Marian thought, 'I hear the same thing from you every week. Why don't
you just resign and let me find someone else, or even do it myself.'

"There really comes a time when we have to be practical. I think
we've more than paid our dues to Miss Evelyn. Enough is enough.
You know what she asked me to do last week?" 'I'm sure you're about
to tell me,' Marian thought. "She wanted me to scrub her kitchen and
bathroom. I'm not supposed to be her charmaid."

'Not that you haven't scrubbed floors before your husband made
his fortune.' "I'm sorry about that. I usually clean the kitchen and bath
on Mondays, and when I can't get around to it, Birdy does it, but this
week I had to get the monthly groceries, and Birdy had to go pick up
a prescription at the drugstore."

"Well, I want to do my part. I didn't mean that, but it just seems to
me we've gotta make some changes."

Marian was relieved that her next call would be to Mabel, the most agreeable woman in town. "You ready for Miss Evelyn on Thursday?"

"Ready as I'll ever be. I'm afraid she's not going to last much longer. I'll miss her. I'll miss my Thursday visits with her."

"You think she's getting weaker?"

"I know so. And grumpier." Mabel laughed with the deep chested chuckle that always made people smile. "Not that she wasn't grumpy before . . . all her life. It tickles me. I get a kick out of it." She chortled again.

Marian laughed with her. "You're a jewel, Mabel. You always make my Sunday afternoons brighter."

The final call was dialed to Cordelia, and Marian sighed as the phone rang. It took Cordelia a while to get to the telephone. Marian wondered if she was in any better shape than Miss Evelyn. Cordelia was in her seventies and crippled with arthritis. Marian wondered if she should still volunteer—she'd hinted that someone else could help out—but Cordelia didn't want to give up her service, and Marian wouldn't insist until she had to. Cordelia was one of the few people who said "Evelyn" rather than "Miss Evelyn." She'd been a member of the church when Miss Evelyn made her bequest.

"Hello?" Cordelia's voice sounded raspy and breathless.

"Hi, Cordelia, it's me, Marian. Are you up to staying with Miss Evelyn this Friday?"

"Far as I can tell. With Evelyn and me it's the halt leading the lame. We get along."

"How do you think she's doing, and how are you doing?"

"Oh, I'm about the same, but she's really failing, you know."

"I worry about you, Cordelia; I don't want you to overdo it."

"I enjoy it. You know Evelyn and I go way back. I remember when she first came here. I thought she was as old as the hills even then. She looked to be in her forties or fifties. Folks were dumbfounded to find out she wasn't even thirty yet. Not that much older than Doris. She never looked different. Never seemed any older than the first time I laid eyes on her . . . until the last year or so."

"How long did she and Doris live together?"

"Close to fifty years, I suppose. Maybe longer. 'Til Doris died. They sorta balanced out one another. Doris so soft and kind and Evelyn so sour and mean."

"Good gracious!"

"No, I shouldn't say that. Evelyn wasn't mean, just strong. She had to be. Lord only knows the women and children she saved. She stood up to drunk husbands and pompous judges and redneck sheriffs and hardboiled county commissioners. She never backed down, and they were all scared to death of her. Evelyn was all no-nonsense, then as now. I really admire that woman. We owe her a lot."

"You're not just talking about the bequest, are you."

"Lord, no, that was the least of it. I'll tell you about that, too, sometime. I was there."

Marian gave George a quick call before she left for Miss Evelyn's house. When he was in town, George received the alarms from the call button that Miss Evelyn wore around her neck. The alarm also went to the fire station and the police department. Most of the time Miss Evelyn would have punched it by mistake, and George would call her and dispatch one of the men of the church before the firemen and the police started out. The firemen and the policemen had gotten tired of all the false alarms, so they'd worked out this system. Someone was always sent from the church, though, because they wanted to be sure Miss Evelyn really was all right, and they needed to reset the call button mechanism. Marian never had to worry about George. He was as organized as she was. If he was going to be away, he would forward the response number to someone else, but she always gave him a quick call on Sunday night after she'd talked with the other volunteers, just to touch base.

WHEN MARIAN RETURNED from Miss Evelyn's house late Monday afternoon, she needed to lie down for an hour before she began preparing Jerry's supper. Jerry had been told several months ago that he'd be getting only a sandwich on Monday nights, but since Marian started giving Miss Evelyn a bath every Monday, she was even more exhausted than before. Mabel gave her a bath every Thursday and even washed her hair every other week, but they'd decided she needed a bath twice a week, although it hardly seemed necessary to Marian—Miss Evelyn seemed immune to sweating and stinking like normal people. Birdy had volunteered to do it, but Miss Evelyn would allow only Mabel and Marian to undress her. Then Birdy assumed most of the shopping. Peggy and Cordelia were asked only to prepare her breakfast and lunch and have food easily accessible for supper, which all of them did, too, and to do any small chores that seemed to be needed or that Miss Evelyn requested.

She ate very little, dry cereal and orange juice and toast for breakfast and whatever the Baptist "Meals on Wheels" delivered for lunch—there was usually plenty left over for her supper and even for the weekend, when no deliveries were made. Miss Evelyn pretended not to know that the meals came from the Baptist Church—she'd said she couldn't swallow food cooked by the Baptists—although she knew very well where it came from.

The first time Marian gave Miss Evelyn a bath she had asked hesitantly if she could keep her glasses on—the big round glasses that made her look like an owl, very different from the little half frame spectacles in all the photographs of her scattered around her house that she wore before her long distance vision began to fail. Marian had never before witnessed Miss Evelyn's vulnerability and almost pathetic dependence as she clung to Marian's arm and even quaked. Undressed, she was so frail and weak that Marian thought of the model airplanes her son Rob had made long ago as a young teenager from thin balsa strips and tissue paper.

Miss Evelyn lived in a house with a big screened porch in front, like many of the older houses on North Main Street. During good weather she enjoyed sitting on the porch with Mabel or Cordelia. She would sometimes sit alone there while Marian attended to chores inside, but she always stayed inside with Birdy and Peggy in order to keep an eye on them. Although the inside rooms were neat and orderly, they were never dusted or swept unless her helpers cleaned them. Doris had done all the light housekeeping before she died—Marian wondered if Miss Evelyn had ever washed a dish in her life—and Doris had employed a cleaning lady who came once a week. The church committee had decided to let the cleaning lady go and do all the housework themselves, so as to save the church that expense.

Every table and chair and even every bureau and chest were covered with the crocheted cloths and knitted afghans that Miss Evelyn had made. When she wasn't working at her job at the Welfare Department, she had knitted and crocheted, as if she had to keep her hands busy and didn't know what else to do with them. Every house in the county must have been given at least one of Miss Evelyn's afghans. She knitted one in pastel colors for each newborn and those in dark colors for older shut-ins. Although she'd given up crocheting, she still knitted incessantly. After she retired she seemed to knit every working hour of the day, although now some of the designs were rather askew and bizarre since her eyesight had declined, even with the powerful owl-like lenses.

What had floored Marian and forced her to a longer rest in bed, however, was neither her usual physical exertions nor the difficulty of giving Miss Evelyn her bath, but rather what she had said just as Marian was leaving. "I hear there's a campaign going on to send me to the nursing home."

"I don't think so, Miss Evelyn. I haven't heard anything like that," Marian had replied, honestly shocked and taken aback.

"Well, Marian, I usually hear about things early. I have a way of sniffing them out—to mix metaphors. If that's what people decide, I'll accept it with as much grace as I can muster. There comes a time when changes have to be made. The good Lord knows I've spent my life making people do what they didn't want to do and oftentimes taking away those they love most, for their own good."

Marian couldn't decide whether to call Peggy, surely the source of the rumor, or to consult Birdy about how to handle it, but in the end she decided to sit on it and tell no one, as hard as that was for her. And so she did until Sunday morning.

HER MIND WANDERED during the sermon. Their old pastor had retired and moved to North Carolina, and the interim minister was not a very compelling preacher. After the service George approached her. "Marian, there's something we need to discuss. Would you be able to drop by my house this afternoon? Or if it's more convenient, I could come to you."

Marian didn't need to ask if it concerned Miss Evelyn. She knew it did. "Why don't I come over to your place right after lunch. About two suit you?"

"Just right. Just right." George's familiarly famous phrase. George was now the Presiding Elder of the Session. With the absence of a regular pastor, the Session would make final decisions about policies, and George would be in charge. 'Thank heavens, George will be in charge,' Marian thought.

George and Lily's home on the outskirts of town was much like George and Lily, a plain and unpretentious brick ranch house on the outside but richly and elegantly furnished on the inside. George and Lily had moved here as a young couple because Lily wanted to live in a small town—"a village," the English would call it. George had commuted to his job at the bank in the county seat. Eventually he became the president of the bank, but now he was retired. They traveled abroad and spent some weekends with their children in the city or at the beach, but mostly they devoted themselves to the church's ministries.

After the usual pleasantries and Cokes with Lily's famous cheese straws, Lily excused herself. "What's all this about, George? Miss Evelyn . . . ?"

George unfolded a letter that Marian had noticed lying ominously on the antique mahogany lamp table beside him—the only thing out of place in the perfectly appointed room. "I've received a petition to the Session asking that Evelyn be placed in a nursing home with the proviso that the church bear all her expenses and that she have the highest quality room, et cetera, et cetera."

"From whom?"

"Peggy, as you might surmise, but signed by a half dozen other members of the congregation."

"Any other women who go every week?"

"No." They were silent for a while. "There's some merit in the idea, Marian, you'll have to admit. There comes a time when we have to make adjustments."

"So Peggy said in so many words . . . and Miss Evelyn, too, remarkably enough." Again there was a silence, about like prayer, more like prayer perhaps than what had taken place during the morning. "Tell me what happened when Miss Evelyn made her bequest. Course I've heard the story a hundred times, but I'd like to hear your version. You were there."

"It was a few year after we moved here and started our family. Lily was pregnant with our second, Lillian. I'd just been elected to the Session. I was the youngest elder—Lily delighted in calling me 'Elder George'. Before we had our first scheduled meeting, an emergency meeting was called. The county engineer had inspected the tower and said it posed an imminent danger. It either had to be repaired or torn down. No services could be held at the church until action was taken. It was the worst crisis we ever faced, at least until, oh, a quarter of a century or so later when we talked about closing the church."

"That's when the Eldridge-Smiths moved here."

"Right."

"Was Miss Evelyn a member of the Session?"

"Oh, no, Evelyn never held any office in the church, so far as I know. Never taught Sunday School or helped with Vacation Bible School or served on a committee. She said she did the Lord's work all week and Sunday was her day of rest. But Doris was an Elder. Doris taught Sunday School and served on half the committees in the church. Evelyn never came to any meetings, except the Session. She always attended the Session with Doris, to find out what all was going on, I suspect. She never attended a committee meeting . . . Oh, I'll take that back.

She did go to the outreach committee when they talked about helping the families on welfare. She and Doris were the Welfare Department for the county, you know—that's what it was called back then, the Welfare Department."

"So she was right there in the meeting."

"Oh, yes. Looking down at her lap crocheting as if she didn't hear a word that was said. Seated behind the elders who were around the table, back off in the corner. They talked and talked. I don't believe I ever said a word. It was my first meeting, you see. Then they decided they'd tear down the tower. It was all they could do. Being constructed of stone, each small piece would have to be taken off and cleaned and fitted and replastered for it to be rebuilt. It would have cost a fortune. There wasn't any money to repair it. I probably had the largest salary of anyone in the church back then, and it was pitiful enough, and Lily and I were just starting out with two babies.

"Old Mr. Harrison, the Presiding Elder, called for the vote, which was unanimous to take down the tower, and all of a sudden Evelyn stood up and flung her crocheting down in the chair and reared back her head and looked at us through those half glasses in that way of hers that could terrify every grown man and wild beast in the county. 'You can't do that,' she said. There was total silence for what seemed like half an hour, though it must have been only a few seconds. 'Miss Evelyn, we can't do no different. We got no money to repair the tower,' Mr. Harrison told her. 'Yes you do,' Evelyn said in that voice of hers that sounded like God Himself was speaking. 'You've got mine. I'll give you my savings to repair the tower. It would be shameful to tear down that tower. It would be like shaving a beautiful woman's head. And while you're at it, there ought to be enough to put a protective shield over the Tiffany window in the chancel. It's more valuable than all the rest of the church property put together, and one good hail storm could take it out.'

"She sat down and began crocheting again. There was another silence that seemed like an hour long. Finally one of the other elders, I forget who now, said, 'But, Miss Evelyn, what will you live on in retirement if you give us all your savings?' Evelyn never looked up from her crocheting. 'I'll have my pension and Social Security. That should suffice.' The other elder, whoever it was, said, 'But, Miss Evelyn, what if you have a major illness or accident.' She still never looked up. 'The church would take care of me,' she said."

"And did the Session make a promise to take care of her, pass a resolution or anything?"

"Nope, not so much as a word was said. It was just understood."

"What do you intend to do, George?"

"That's why I wanted to talk things over with you and see if you agreed to how I plan to handle it. I thought I'd schedule the discussion for a regular meeting of the Session. I don't want to call an emergency meeting. I want you and all her regular helpers to be there and share your thoughts. Of course, I can't ask just certain people to come, so it will have to be open to everyone. I know the rules say all Session meetings are open to any member of the congregation, but I mean this needs to be announced and publicized so anyone who wants to come, can come and say their piece. How does that sound to you, Marian?"

"It sounds to me like just the right way to proceed."

"You know I've got to remain impartial. I can't take sides."

"I know, but you're one of the few people who knows what really happened when she gave her bequest. I learned so much I didn't know—sort of got a feeling for what it was like—when you told the story of it just now."

"You need to talk to Lloyd. He was an Elder on the Session back then with me. And Cordelia. She wasn't on the Session at that particular time, but she knows more about the history of this place than anyone else who's still living. There're not many of us left, as you said. Those are the only two I can thing of who could really shed some light on things. Mabel might remember certain things, too."

"I'll call them right away."

"I'd prefer you wait until after I make the announcement next Sunday. The regular meeting of the Session is already scheduled for the following Sunday evening."

IT WAS HARD FOR MARIAN not to talk with anyone about it during the week. The more she thought about it, the more she was convinced that Birdy was involved in the "campaign," as Miss Evelyn had put it. Peggy would not have taken that kind of dramatic initiative without some kind of encouragement from Birdy.

Although Marian had intended talking first with Lloyd, she saw Mabel coming out of the service on Sunday morning, visibly upset. "They just can't do that to that poor old woman. I'm not going to stand for it. I'll leave the church, if they put her in the nursing home."

"Why don't I drop by your house this afternoon so we can talk about it."

"I'd appreciate that a whole lot, Marian."

Mabel lived in one of the houses in the cotton mill village that had been sold to workers at a discount when the mill closed. She'd added a deck on the side and a new entrance porch and put in flower beds along the sidewalk and flower boxes on the front windows, so that it didn't look like the other houses on the street, which were once so much alike that you had to read the number on the curb to be sure you were at the right address.

Marian let Mabel ventilate for a while before responding to her. "It just isn't right. This town owes a lot to that old lady, not just the church because of her bequest. There's no accounting for all the children she saved. I know some of who they were, though I'm not telling any names. She and Miss Doris were the Welfare Department, you know. Miss Doris came in straight out of college to help Miss Evelyn. She was a few years younger, not that much difference in their ages, though. What a pair! Miss Doris was soft and sweet. She had soft wavy brown hair that she wore loose and was always smiling. Miss Evelyn had short tight curls and always seemed to be scowling. People could talk Miss Doris into anything. She fell for their stories about being sorry and never doing it again. Not Miss Evelyn. You couldn't pull the wool over her eyes. She never learned to drive, you know. Miss Doris had to drive her out in the county when they had to call on a family in trouble. It's just not fair, Marian. It's not right to do that after all she's given us."

"I've talked to George a little about it. As I understand it, there are three main concerns—whether Miss Evelyn is getting the proper care she needs, what's the best stewardship of our financial resources to support her, and whether there's too great a burden on our volunteers."

"And that last part is the clincher, I believe."

"All the more reason for you and me to tell our view of things at the meeting next Sunday."

"Marian, you know I can't speak in public, but I'll be there, and I might just have to speak up in spite of myself."

While she was in the mill village Marian decided to stop by Lloyd's house in case he was home. It was at the far end of the village down the hill from Mabel's house, with the other small shotgun houses built for the line workers, much smaller than the houses like Mabel's built for employees in the office. Lloyd and his wife had bought the house they were living in, as Mabel had bought hers, when the mill closed. For a while Lloyd managed a gas station. Then he worked in the produce section at the grocery store. Now he lived on his Social Security check. Unlike Mabel's freshly painted house, Lloyd's house had peeling paint and several rotten boards next to the front steps and more weeds than sparse grass in the yard. Since his wife died Marian had noticed that Lloyd sometimes arrived at church dressed in clothes that needed laundering. Several minutes after she knocked, Marian heard Lloyd stumbling to the door.

"Miss Marian, please do come in. I was taking my Sunday afternoon nap. I hope you wasn't there too long."

"Not at all. I'm sorry I got you up."

"I sleep plenty. Before long it'll be full time, as they say."

The inside of Lloyd's house was as pathetic as the outside. Marian thought the church needed to give Lloyd some attention and schedule a fix-up day for him. Between the two worn, stained recliners facing the television set was a folding tray with metal legs. There were no lamps in the room, just the overhead ceiling fixture. Several old straight chairs with plaited denim strip seats were scattered around the room. A beautiful antique sideboard sat against the wall.

"That's a beautiful sideboard, Lloyd. It must have a story connected to it."

"That was inherited from my wife's family. They say it's over two hundred years old. I think a whole lot of it . . . reminds me of her." Lloyd dropped his head, and Marian thought he might weep, but his eyes remained dry.

"She was a lovely woman. I know you miss her."

"Yes'um. We never had no children, you know. Now that Sally's gone and my mother and aunt that died a whole long time ago, all's I got left is Miss Evelyn. I reckin that's why you're here."

"You heard about the meeting for next Sunday at church today. I wanted to learn what Miss Evelyn was like before I knew her."

"Things was rough when Miss Evelyn first come here. There was a bunch of men in the village what got drunk and beat their wives most every weekend. When Miss Evelyn got wind of it, she had the sheriff haul 'em off to jail right regular, and that pretty soon put a stop to it, after a while."

Lloyd paused, and Marian waited for him to go on, because it seemed he had something else to say. "That's very helpful for me to know, Lloyd. Thank you."

"That ain't all. Some of the men started in to beating up on their children when Miss Evelyn stopped them from beating up on their wives. They was some that sexually abused children. Miss Evelyn come in and snatched up them children and wouldn't let those men anywhere back close to 'em." Lloyd paused, but this time Marion didn't interrupt him. "I know. I was one of them children."

"Lloyd." Evelyn's voice was quiet, almost prayerful.

"You ever wondered why I wear these here long sleeve shirts all the time. It's to hide the scars from the cigarette burns I got on my arms from my daddy. I never told nobody about that before, excepting Sally, but if an' it helps Miss Evelyn, I'll just roll up my sleeves at the meetin' and let ever'body look at 'em."

"You won't have to do that, Lloyd. I'm sure."

"Peggy's family they lived down the street from us. Her pa and my daddy was best friends. Daddy convinced them I was a liar, and I reckin they believe it yet."

"That explains a lot."

"Well, that still ain't all. Miss Evelyn took me to live with my grand-mother and my aunt. Mama could come see me whenever she wanted to, and she did most every single day, but Daddy he could only come visit if Miss Evelyn was there, too, and that didn't happen very often, for which I thank the good Lord."

"Was your grandmother a member of the Presbyterian Church?"

"Oh, Lordy, no. You ever wonder why there's so many mill folks members of the Presbyterian Church? Miss Evelyn and Miss Doris would go around and gather up children on Sunday mornings and take 'em to Miss Doris's Sunday School class. Before that they was all Baptists, what went to church at all."

"I understand Miss Doris was a lovely person, too."

"She was a real sweet lady. She taught me about love and being nice and Jesus an' all, but it was Miss Evelyn what saved my life."

MARIAN WAS limp with exhaustion when she left Lloyd's house, and she decided she couldn't talk with anyone else that afternoon, but she still had to make her usual calls to set up the week. She felt she had to say something about the meeting to Peggy, Birdy, and Cordelia.

"Peggy, I understand you signed the petition to discuss changes in Miss Evelyn's care."

"I thought it was about time to re-evaluate things. You know a lot of you newcomers think she's a saint, but there are some people in this town that think she's as mean as a snake."

Marian almost said, 'I visited with Lloyd this afternoon,' but thought better of it and caught herself. "What does Birdy think about the peti-tion? I imagine you mentioned it to her."

"I believe she's all for it, 'though she said she couldn't sign it, I sup-pose because she's so new to town."

Marian didn't know what to say to Birdy. She was angered by her suspicion that Birdy had manipulated Peggy to send the petition and frustrated and saddened that Birdy had not confided in her. She decided to be direct. "Birdy, did you know about that petition?"

"Yeah, I knew about it from the start."

"Did you have anything to do with drafting it?"

"I gave Peggy a few ideas, yeah."

"Birdy, I thought we were friends. Why didn't you mention it to me?"

"Honey, you're probably the best friend I've ever had in the world. I wanted to spare you. I didn't want to get you involved."

"Well, I'm really . . . peeved." It was not the word Marian wanted to use. "I'm really upset with you, Birdy."

"Let's wait and see how this all comes out. Then we can talk it through. I'll take you down to the beach house, and we can hash through every glorious detail."

"I don't think so, Birdy. I'm really angry at you."

"I'm sorry. Wait and see. Just wait and see what happens first, OK?"

MARIAN HAD TOLD CORDELIA on the phone Sunday afternoon that she wanted to talk with her, but they'd agreed it would be best to wait until after Cordelia's visit with Miss Evelyn on Friday. On Saturday morning Marian drove into the circle in front of Cordelia's beautiful old home, one of the oldest houses in town. It was a simple raised cottage, but its elegance couldn't be duplicated by any of the mansions in Birdy's gated neighborhood. Marian told Cordelia about her visit with Lloyd and her conversation with Peggy. She didn't mention her conversation with Birdy. She was surprised to learn that Cordelia knew all about the childhoods of Lloyd and Peggy. "Lloyd was about the sweetest little boy who ever lived, and he's one of the sweetest men, as you well know, and his father was one of the meanest men I ever knew. I guess maybe Evelyn was mean. Sometimes it takes mean to know mean."

THE SUN was setting as Marian drove toward the Presbyterian Church on Sunday afternoon. The little tan stones glowed like mosaics with red and yellow brilliance up to the point on the steeple of the tower below the exquisitely carved Celtic cross—the cross that had been added to the steeple's tower when it had been repaired, also from Miss Evelyn's bequest and according to her suggestion for its design.

The Baptists had torn down their nineteenth-century building and erected a brick structure that looked like most newer Baptist churches, in the architectural style that Birdy called "Baptist miniature colonial." The Methodists still worshipped in their charming old clapboard building. Episcopalians, despite several attempts over the decades, could never muster enough members to construct a building, and the four or five Episcopal families had to drive to the county seat or even into the city to worship. There used to be only one or two Catholic families who had to drive into the county seat to their parish, and the Catholics still had to go there, even with the influx of Hispanic workers who worked at Harold's chicken processing plant, because the Roman Catholic Church didn't have enough priests to establish a new parish. The Presbyterian Church really was the jewel of the town, even sur-passing the beauty of old homes like Cordelia's, and the tower was its crowning glory, like the beautiful hair of a beautiful woman, as Miss Evelyn had put it long ago.

Marian deliberately chose a seat across the room from Birdy. As usual Birdy was immaculate in her tailored dress like the fashionable sport clothes she always wore. It probably cost more than everything in Marian's closet. The wedding reception for Birdy's daughter had been the only time Marian had ever seen her in a formal dress. Her daughter's wedding dress had been hand made in Italy with pearls sewn into the bodice, according to the newspapers. Birdy refused to tell where her dress had come from. As Cordelia had said, the mother and daughter could have taken the prize in any fashion magazine in the world. Birdy was a truly beautiful woman, but tonight Marian didn't feel much admiration for her.

George called the meeting to order and described the agenda as falling into three categories—the proper care for Miss Evelyn, the availability and willingness of volunteers, and financial considerations.

"Since I'm an old banker, you might guess that I'd put money first on the agenda, and I've asked our treasurer, Bob Lawson, to crunch some numbers for us."

Bob was a young banker who wanted to impress George by assembling greater details and figures than anyone in the room had any interest in hearing about, but his report had the effect of calming emotions and putting things into perspective as people became more and more bored. The bottom line was that even though the nursing home would be considerably more expensive than the present arrangement, Medicaid payments would pick up much of the difference, since she'd exhausted her assets, and according to federal rules, Miss Evelyn's house, which everyone knew was to be left to the church under her present will, wouldn't have to be sold and could be rented to make up the rest of the difference in her nursing home expenses, so that it would be something of a wash either way financially.

When Bob sat down, George said, "Just right. Just right. Thanks, Bob. And now I'd like for Marian to speak as the coordinator of the volunteers."

Marian was surprised that she was so emotional that her voice quavered. She said that she couldn't speak for all the volunteers—she hadn't canvassed them all—but that she believed most of them would be willing and eager to continue their help with Miss Evelyn. "Let me add personally that even though the nursing home would meet Miss Evelyn's medical and physical needs and might be able to do certain things a little better than we can, I believe we're taking good care of her, and allowing her the privacy of staying in her own home with the love and personal attention we give her adds a quality to her life that the nursing home simply cannot supply."

As she was sitting down, Marian realized she was quaking. George smiled at her and blinked his eyes. "Thanks, Marian. Just right. Just right. And thank you for all you and the ladies of the church do . . . for Miss Evelyn and for all of us. Now I'd like for Lloyd to say a few words on behalf of the men who help out."

Lloyd repeated much of the story he'd shared with Marian about drunken men beating their wives and abusing their children, although he never referred explicitly to himself and his family nor did he mention the cigarette burns on his arms. Even so, his testimony powerfully affected many people, who dabbed at their eyes. Some men reached into their back pockets and pulled out their handkerchiefs and pretended to blow their noses while furtively staunching their tears.

"Anybody else want to say something?" George paused and looked around the room. "Well then, I guess we're ready for a vote. The Session will make the final decision, of course, but as Presiding Elder, I think I can promise that what the congregation favors will be a primary consideration."

Suddenly Birdy raised her hand. "Before we vote I'd just like to say whatever ya'll decide to do, I plan to spend as much time as ever with Miss Evelyn on my day every week, no matter where she's at. She's a tough old"—Marian shot Birdy a warning glance across the room—"lady."

"That goes double for me." Mabel's voice trembled emotionally.

"And certainly for me as well." Cordelia nodded and grasped Mabel's hand beside her.

Peggy stammered and stuttered in an unprepared and unanticipated speech. "You all know I'll go see Miss Evelyn and do what I can to help take care of her just as long . . . forever . . . just as Mrs. Ethridge-Smith said . . . me, too. I didn't mean that we should abandon her. You know . . . I just thought we ought to clarify things and evaluate . . ." Marian observed that Birdy had not quite toned down Peggy's mascara enough to keep it from running onto her cheeks now. At least she no longer wore eyeliner and eye shadow like an opera prima donna.

"And we're really grateful to you, Peggy, for suggesting that we review things," Birdy smiled at the bewildered Peggy as she spoke.

"Yes, thanks, Peggy. You did us all a real service by bringing things to our attention." George also smiled benignly at the increasingly disoriented Peggy.

The vote was unanimous to continue assisting Miss Evelyn in her home. As the meeting was breaking up Marian saw Birdy walk over toward Lloyd, and Marian moved closer to overhear their conversation. "That was some swell speech, Lloyd. I loved it. I have to ask you a favor, though."

"Anything you say, Miss Robin."

"I really, really want you to call me 'Birdy.'"

"That'ud be right hard, Miss . . ."

"But you'll do it for me, won't you, Lloyd? I really want you to."

"OK . . . Birdy."

"We gotta get together more often. We won't tell my husband about it." Birdy bowed and grinned her infectious smile and kissed Lloyd on the cheek. "I really do love you, Lloyd." He blushed deep crimson like an infatuated adolescent.

Then Birdy headed toward Marian, who was loaded for bear and waiting for her. "What in God's name did you mean by putting us through all this, Birdy?"

"Did you notice Miss Evelyn's legacy tonight?"

"Yes, the tower was absolutely glorious in the sunset as I drove up, but what the hell does that have to do with anything?"

"That's not Miss Evelyn's real legacy. It's right here in this room. Just look at these people. We wouldn't give each other the time of day if it wasn't for her. Do you suppose she planned it that way, or did it just happen?"

"I have no idea. I'm just furious with you. Why did you have to do things this way for Christ's sake?"

"Marian, you've cussed more in the last two minutes than I've ever heard in all our years together . . . Because it was time to renew our covenant vows. See, I don't just think about my golf game in church all the time. Sometimes I pick up on the religious lingo."

"Birdy, I don't know. I'm still exasperated with you."

"We're still friends, aren't we?"

"Yes, of course we are."

"And you'll still come on down to the beach house with me week after next, won't you?"

"I don't know. I'll see if I can fit it into my schedule."

"You really are the best friend I ever had, Marian. I really do love you."

"I love you, too, Birdy."

"And I really do love that tough old bitch. Now I've gone and said it."

www.ingramcontent.com/pod-product-compliance
Lightning Source LLC
Chambersburg PA
CBHW022025090426
42739CB00006BA/290